OTHER Products BY TRAILER LIFE

RV Handbook - 3rd Edition
This "no fluff" comprehensive guide for both novice and seasoned RVers has thousands across the U.S. and Canada reaching for this book as a constant source of reference. It has become the "bible" for the RV road warrior. Features hundreds of proven RV tips, tricks and techniques to save you time, money and maybe even your sanity. Packed with user-friendly technical advice, checklists, schematics, photos and charts. You simply won't find this level of detail covered in any other RV book.
8½ x 10¾, 275 pages
ISBN: 0-934798-66-4
$29.95 plus $4.25 shipping and handling

Trailer Life's RV Repair & Maintenance Manual, Fourth Edition
Bob Livingston
This revised edition presents recreational vehicle owners with all the practical knowledge needed for diagnosing problems, making repairs, and communicating with mechanics. Filled with detailed troubleshooting guides and checklists, hundreds of comprehensive illustrations and photographs, and easy-to-understand step-by-step instructions for repairing, replacing, and maintaining systems.
8½ x 11, 500 pages
ISBN: 0-934798-70-2
$34.95 plus $4.25 shipping and handling

10-Minute Tech
Here are hundreds of easy-to-do, money-saving tips taken from Trailer Life Magazine's "10-Minute Tech"– the most widely read and talked-about self-help column for RVers. This handy book features clever ways to help you improve the RV's livability, plenty of towing tips and procedures for cleaning and maintaining the rig, user-friendly tips on fixing your appliances, great ideas for storage and much more. Filled with easy to follow illustrations that will help turn RVers into savvy do-it-yourselfers.
7¾ x 9½, 219 pages
ISBN: 0-934798-59-1
$29.95 plus $4.25 shipping and handling

10-Minute Tech, Volume 2
Turn yourself into a savvy do-it-yourselfer with 600 all-new, ten-minute solutions – to fix every maddening RV problem imaginable! Here are even more easy-to-do, money-saving ideas from Trailer Life and MotorHome magazine's "Quick Tips" self-help column for RVers, written by RVers. On page after page of the all new 10 Minute Tech - Volume 2, there are hundreds of fantastic, nuisance-saving tips. Great money-saving ideas. Super time-saving inventions. Amazing good sense. Savvy short-cuts. And neat little tricks to make your RVing easier, safer, and more fun!
7¾ x 9½, 168 pages
ISBN: 0-934798-72-9
$29.95 plus $4.25 shipping and handling

Continued overleaf

10-Minute Tech, Volume 3

This all new volume, the latest release in the popular "10-Minute Tech" book series, offers readers a collection of simple, handy tips submitted to the popular self-help columns "10-Minute Tech" in Trailer Life magazine and "Quick Tips" in MotorHome magazine. RVers share over 600 more of their clever, user-friendly solutions for maximizing storage space, cleaning, towing, safety and livability. Whether you are into mobile computing, barbequing or just keeping your vehicle in tip-top shape, you are guaranteed to find ingenious, money saving ideas in this full-color book.
7¾ x 9½, 174 pages
$29.95 plus $4.25 shipping and handling
ISBN: 0-934798-80-X

Complete Guide to Full-time RVing: Life on the Open Road, Third Edition
Bill and Jan Moeller

This best-selling how-to-do-it book covers a broad range of subjects of interest to full-timers, those considering a full-time lifestyle, or seasonal RVers. New and expanded chapters including working full-timers, remodeling your RV for full-time living, and widebody RVs, in addition to chapters on costs, choosing the right RV, safety and security, and more.
7⅜ x 9¼, 548 pages
$29.95 plus $4.25 shipping and handling
ISBN: 0-934798-53-2

These books are available at fine bookstores everywhere. Or, you may order directly from Trailer Life Books. For each book ordered, simply send us the name of the book, the price, and shipping and handling (California residents please add appropriate sales tax).

Mail orders to:
Trailer Life Books
64 Inverness Drive East
Englewood, CO 80112

You may call our customer-service representatives if you wish to charge your order or if you want more information. Please phone, toll-free, Monday through Friday, 6:30 A.M. to 6:30 P.M.; Saturday, 7:30 A.M. to 1:30 P.M., Mountain Time, 1-800-766-1674.

Or, Visit us online at www.TrailerLifeDirectory.com

Pet E.R. Guide

A Directory of 24-Hour and After-Hour Veterinary Facilities in the United States

By Melinda Lord

From the Editors of Trailer Life Books

TRAILER
LIFE
BOOKS

Affinity Group, Inc.

Pet E.R.
Guide
By Melinda Lord
Trailer Life Books

Group Publisher: Joe Daquino

Associate Publisher: Cindy Halley

Senior Director of Production: Christine Bucher

Production Manager: Carol Sankman

Senior Director of Marketing: Kim Souza

Direct Mail Manager: Ellen Tyson

Internet Marketing Manager: Samantha Price

Proofreader: Tino Velasvo

Book Design: Robert George/Direct Design

Published by Trailer Life Books, TL Enterprises, Inc., Ventura, California.
A wholly owned subsidiary of Affinity Group, Inc.

Printed in the United States of America

Library of Congress Cataloging-in-Publication Data is available upon request.
ISBN 978-0-934798-89-1

10 9 8 7 6 5 4 3 2 1

www.TrailerLifeDirectory.com

Disclaimer

The intent of this book is to provide additional information to pet owners so that they may evaluate options in the event veterinary assistance may be needed.

This book does not endorse any provider of service, nor is its intent to recommend any provider of service. It is up to the consumer to research and decide what is best for them. We have not checked provider qualifications, licensing, or quality of care. The reader must use their own resources in any decision making process.

The intent of this book is to simply provide the reader with a helpful guide and contact information for possibly available 24-Hour and/or After-Hour veterinary service facilities. The information provided has been compiled from publicly available sources. Although it contains hundreds of facilities across the United States, it should not be considered to be complete.

For example, this book may not list the numerous "normal business hours" for veterinarians who may be available in an emergency, or who are on-call after hours. Therefore, please understand that this publication is intended to acquaint you with what may be available in the areas in which you are traveling. It is up to you to confirm the information for its current accuracy.

Table of Contents

* with permission from the *American Society for the Prevention of Cruelty to Animals* (ASPCA)

Pet E.R. Guide

Dedication

This book is dedicated to a variety of people (and puppies) who have lovingly supported me during its creation.

To my wonderful husband, who encouraged me and helped me. You never minded the fact that I kept my nose in front of the computer screen to work on this project. You are great!

To my mom, who enthusiastically helped proof sections and shuffled many papers to make this a reality. You can go back to quilting for the Humane Society animals now, as well as work with your other charities.

To my 'kids', my four-legged pups, you are the best! I hope we make you as happy as you make us! You sure are loved!

To Bubba, may this be a gift that I can give others. You are an angel.

To my dad and other family members in heaven, may you smile upon those who may benefit from this publication. I know you are there to help all of us.

And, to all the others who encouraged me in the creation and development of this book, including my sister, nephew, friends, and neighbors.

With additional thanks to "Doc F" and "C.N.", and to all who helped make this a reality.

Thank you!

Pet E.R. Guide

Some Special Comments

Important

PLEASE, PLEASE, PLEASE CALL the facility you plan to visit *before* transporting your pet there. Veterinary emergency facilities are businesses. Businesses go "out of business", get sold, change addresses, change names, change phone numbers/area codes, and change hours. Make sure you get up-to-date information for the facility when you call so that you make the most of every moment. If you find the facility is no longer available, you can immediately seek another facility to contact.

Although we have captured a variety of locations within each state, there are definitely some states that have limited options for veterinary emergency facilities that are open nights, weekends, holidays, or 24 hours. *Please understand that it is always your choice to call any practicing veterinarian you can reach within your current locale.* Some local veterinarians will have 'on call service', while others do not.

Pet E.R. Guide

Chapter One

Our Experience

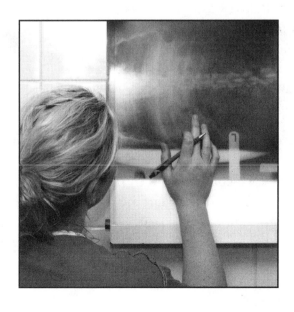

Chapter One

Our Experience

This book is for all pet owners. We sincerely hope that you never have to find emergency care for your pet. However, we have created this book to provide some guidance and comfort of hope if your pet requires medical assistance while you are away from your regular veterinarian.

Some six years ago, we were on a long weekend away from our home with our beautiful cocker spaniel, our little furry angel, Bubba. On Saturday, we all spent some time relaxing, sitting in front of the television, and walking on the beach. The day was beautiful, and the sun from the April sky was warming as we felt spring was soon to give way to summer.

Bubba

Shortly after we finished dinner it seemed that Bubba was acting as though something was wrong. The symptoms he was displaying led us to think that perhaps his stomach wasn't feeling very well, as he had a previous issue with his digestive system the prior year.

Worried, we called a local veterinarian's number and had to leave a message. They returned our call promptly, however they did not seem all that concerned and they felt we could wait until the next day to bring our pet in for an exam. They nicely redirected us to another veterinarian that might help us in the next town. They also informed us that this facility was not staffed around the clock. And if, by chance, Bubba had to be hospitalized, he would be there by himself until someone came in on Sunday morning to feed the pets that were hospitalized or boarded for the night.

Given the option of leaving our dog overnight was heart-wrenching. We were afraid he would feel abandoned and scared, and we were not comfortable leaving him alone.

We discussed our options and the initial reaction from the first veterinarian we spoke with. Keeping that all in mind, we felt that we may have been overreacting and decided to wait and see if Bubba would feel better in the morning. If he still wasn't feeling well we would immediately go to the 24-Hour veterinary clinic near our home.

When we woke up Sunday morning, incredibly and sadly, we found that he had passed away in his sleep. The shock and disbelief we felt that day is difficult to describe. It is a decision that still breaks our hearts today. Our little Bubba, then an angel on earth, is now our angel in heaven, and we miss him.

That was our first time away from home where a need for a veterinarian surfaced.

In the year after Bubba's passing, my wonderful dad also became ill and passed away. I remember my dad and mom just loved Bubba. When we visited, he would be at my mom's feet in the kitchen looking for a treat or two or would accompany my dad to the bathroom to 'keep him company'. It was quite cute! It is comforting to know that my dad and our Bubba are both in heaven, but the feeling still lingers that maybe we could have done something more. (We always feel like we should be as helpful as we can, despite the futility of some things. With my dad, we pretty much knew it was out of our hands, but with Bubba, it felt as though we missed an opportunity to help him.)

During the year that followed, the thought of getting another dog didn't really cross our minds. It was just too painful to think about and, simply, we just weren't ready. But, as we entered a second year without Bubba, my wonderful husband and I started talking about different breeds of dogs. We'd watch dog shows and competitions on television, learning more about the variety of dog breeds and their characteristics. We were just 'learning', not buying.

One day when we had nothing to do (a rarity), we decided to drive to a place recommended to us where we could see and interact with a few different dog breeds. We figured we would learn more about some of the breeds we had been researching for some time. Little did we know we would not only get one dog, but we would come home with two dogs that day! Two darling Shih Tzu mixes that we lovingly call "The Kids".

Although not brother and sister, they are very close, and they quickly became our 'children' too! My mom thinks of them as her 'grandchildren', whom she adores. My sister now has a 'niece' and a 'nephew' (the only ones), and she spoils them accordingly. My nephew has two 'cousins'. And, my father-in-law, not generally comfortable with dogs, has come to really enjoy them. But, as far as 'mom' and 'dad', you can bet we love 'em! When you love your pets they are part of your family. These two little ones are great, and we travel everywhere with them.

They got initiated to 'road trips' from the day we picked them up and drove them home. Given our enjoyment of travel, and visiting new places, it was great to see them adapt to that kind of life. Somehow, we'd like to think they enjoy it too!

The 'kids'

While we began our family trips in a car, a few years back we bought a recreational vehicle (RV) and that is how we mainly travel with them now. Being smaller dogs, it is easy to travel and exist in limited space while in our RV. However, we have seen many larger dogs on the road with their owners in a wide variety of vehicles too. But dogs aren't the only pets we see in our travels. We see a variety of pet owners with their cats, birds, and other companion animals as well.

What we all have in common with people who *are* traveling with pets are the same things we have in common with other people who *are not* traveling with pets. That is … we are in a place that is not home. The surroundings are new and different, and the familiarity of where to go to locate stores, gas, hospitals, and doctors or veterinarians are all foreign to us. However, the likelihood of finding a grocery store or gas station is fairly good, as the odds are that just driving a short distance will lead you to one. Hospitals, while not as abundant, are usually clearly marked on well traveled roads, or you can pretty much count on the local population to tell you where you can find one. Unfortunately though, when it comes to veterinarians, it isn't that easy.

While there is certainly the opportunity to find a veterinarian in your travels, the options can become narrow. There are veterinarians that are open daily during normal business hours. Some have their regular clientele, and are happy to treat new pets. Some have their regular clientele, but do not take any new pets. Some offices take emergency phone calls after hours, but are not in the office. Some offices have their emergency calls routed to other veterinarians on call. In a nutshell, all of this is commendable but an emergency that can happen during the day becomes much more frightening at night, or on a weekend, when veterinary help isn't as abundant or available.

Why is it that emergencies always seem to occur in the middle of the night, on a holiday, or when you are away from home? You are caught in a panic to help your family pet and companion, without the comfort of knowing your surroundings or where to turn. Having felt that way years ago with Bubba, we had hoped that the feeling of panic, being in a strange place, and facing a possible pet emergency, would not ever happen again. However, it did, and recently! We needed veterinary assistance for one of our newest family members, our 'little boy'.

We were vacationing in an area where driving a distance seemed to be the norm in order to get any place. Having had a quiet day reading, relaxing, and playing with our two 'kids', we found ourselves in a situation that brought us some concern. It was in the early evening that one of our dogs seemed very quiet, and somewhat uncomfortable. Considering he is the little comedian of the two, it was odd to see him look so serious and to see him panting the way he was. Nothing out of the ordinary occurred that day, so we couldn't figure out what was going on. We waited a while to see if he was just tired and hot, or if he was ill. Thinking that he may need to see a vet, we decided to seek out some help.

After a little research we found a local veterinarian and placed a call that evening, reaching him at his home. The vet didn't think his condition sounded too serious, but we were still concerned. We placed a call to our regular veterinarian, described our situation, and explained that we were out of town. He seemed to mirror our concern and thought the symptom could indicate the possibility of a slipped disc, however, it could be nothing. He recommended that he be seen that night. Having erred on the wrong side of that years ago, it was too frightening to take a chance on our little guy.

Our veterinarian from home told us to contact the local veterinarian again and ask where a 24-Hour vet was located so we could bring him in that evening. We made the call, and the veterinarian told us that the closest 24-Hour vet was at least a couple of hours away. He offered to open his office if we wanted him to see our dog that night. Given our concern at this point, and the fact that much of the evening had been consumed shuttling phone calls back and forth, we indicated that we would meet him at his office. The drive to his office was still a distance away.

We got there and waited for him to arrive. After the veterinarian examined him, it was determined that he had a pulled muscle in his leg. We were grateful that a steroid injection was all that was needed to alleviate our dog's discomfort, and ours too.

All in all, it would have been much better if we had more complete information on the veterinary facilities within the area we were visiting. We would have been able to determine what our options were early on and decide what we wanted to do in a more timely manner. On this occasion, it was uncomfortable to ask this veterinarian to leave his home to come to the office, but neither my husband or I, or our regular veterinarian from home, felt that it was appropriate to let this go until the morning.

We were fortunate that, medically, it all turned out well. Our veterinarian back home checked him out a few days later when we returned, and all was fine. However, the process that we had gone though to get to that point was still difficult.

It was really after this event that the idea to put together a compilation of emergency veterinary hospitals came to be. Initially it was for our own use, but it became apparent that other pet owners could benefit from having this information as well.

As we indicated, we hope you never have reason to utilize any emergency medical treatment for your pet. But, if you do, we hope this directory might bring you a feeling of hope and peace of mind, while acting as a guide to help you explore your medical options in order to help your family pet.

Pet E.R. Guide

Chapter Two

Emergency Veterinary Locations

Suggestions and Reminders

Directory of Emergency Veterinary Facilities
State by State Listing

Chapter Two

Suggestions & Reminders

FOR YOU AND YOUR PET

Before proceeding to any facility listed in this book, or anywhere else, FIRST call the provider you plan to visit before you leave with your pet.

Make sure the practice:

1) is still in business providing services your pet needs.
2) is still located at the same street address.
3) is still located in the same town* or city*.
4) will be open at the time you expect to arrive with your pet.

Directions

Additionally, ask for directions from where you will be coming from. If you are not familiar with the area, getting directions to get you there most efficiently is imperative to getting there in the most expedient way possible.

* Sometimes facilities associate themselves with the larger city name when they are located in a suburb, and sometimes they associate themselves with the neighboring town they are actually in.

FOR THE EMERGENCY FACILITY, YOU, AND YOUR PET

"Call First" ...

... is a request of many of the emergency facilities listed in this directory. This enables the facility to prepare for your pet's arrival based on the pet's medical condition and situation. It also enables the facility to tell you what you might be able to do to help your pet's condition on the way to the facility. Depending on the severity of the situation, there are some facilities that have pet ambulances available. Feel free to ask.

Payment of Services

Since any facility in this directory is unlikely to be your pet's primary care veterinarian, it is wise to be prepared for the way the facility wishes to be paid for their services (cash, check, debit card, charge cards).

In researching different facilities, we came across veterinary clinics that took Care Credit®, a pre-approved credit payment lender. You can learn more on their website www.carecredit.com to see if it is right for you.

Emergency Veterinary Facility State by State Listing

This Directory of Emergency Veterinary Facilities, State by State Listing, has been compiled based on a variety of publicly available resources and includes our own extensive inquiries.

While documentation of many of these facilities began from these searches, information for our own personal use, most times, confirmed information or we sought additional information directly from the facility itself. As such, information for each facility may have come from various places, and was compiled for our personal use as well as for this publication.

You will notice that there are certain cities, and towns that are spelled out in capital letters. These are locations where a veterinary school of higher education is located. Services available may be limited or extensive, and, like any provider of service in this book, may vary or change at any point in time.

All in all, this directory is a labor of hope.

ALABAMA

Anniston - *Calhoun County*
Animal Medical Center of Anniston
719 Quintard Avenue
Anniston, AL 36201
Phone: (256) 236-8387
Fax: --
Website: www.amcvets.com
Hours: 24 hours a day;
      7 days a week;
      365 days a year

AUBURN - *Lee County*
Auburn University
College of Veterinary Medicine
Auburn University Small Animal
   Teaching Hospital
1185 Wire Road
Auburn, AL 36849
Phone: (334) 844-4690
Fax: (334) 844-6034
Website: www.vetmed.auburn.edu
Note: Call to discuss emergency.

Birmingham - *Jefferson County*
Alabama Veterinary Specialists
3783 Pine Lane SE
Birmingham, AL 35022
Phone: (205) 481-1001
Fax: (205) 428-8704
Website:
www.alabamaveterinaryspecialists.com
Hours: 24 hours a day;
     7 days a week

Emergency Pet Care Clinic
4524 Southlake Parkway - Suite 28
Birmingham, AL 35244
Phone: (205) 988-5988
Fax: (205) 988-5935
Website: --
Hours: 24 hours a day;
     7 days a week

Emergency & Specialty
   Animal Medical Clinic/
   Emergency Pet Care Clinic
2864 Acton Road
Birmingham, AL 35243
ER Phone: (205) 967-7389
Phone 1: (205) 967-9107
Phone 2: (205) 967-9184
Fax: --
Website: --
Hours: 24 hours a day

Miles

Florence - *Lauderdale County*
Florence Veterinary Emergency Clinic
205 South Seminary Street - Suite 222
Florence, AL 35630
Phone: (256) 740-8206
Fax: (256) 740-8203
Website: --
Hours: 24 hours a day

Huntsville - *Madison County*
Animal Emergency Clinic of
   North Alabama (AEC)
2112 Memorial Parkway SW
Huntsville, AL 35801
Phone: (256) 533-7600
Fax 1: (256) 533 7611
Fax 2: (256) 533-7610
Website: --
Hours: Mon - Fri (6pm-8am);
     Weekends from Fri (6pm) -
     Mon (8am); Holidays

Montgomery - *Montgomery County*
Animal Emergency Clinic
1500 West Street
Montgomery, AL 36106
Phone: (334) 264-5555
Fax: --
Website: --
Hours: Mon - Fri (6pm-8am);
       Weekends from Sat (noon) -
       Mon (8am)

Oxford - *Calhoun County*
Animal Medical Center of Anniston
225 Plaza Lane
Oxford, AL 36203
Phone: (256) 832-8387
Fax: --
Website: www.amcvets.com
Hours: 24 hours a day;
       7 days a week;
       365 days a year

TUSKEGEE - *Macon County*
Tuskegee University
College of Veterinary Medicine,
    Nursing, & Allied Health
Tuskegee, AL 36088
Phone: (344) 727-8174 Main Number
Phone: (334) 727-8436 Hospital
Fax: (334) 727-8177
Website: www.tuskegee.edu
Hours: Emergency services are
       available 24 hours a day. Call.

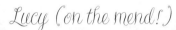

Lucy (on the mend!)

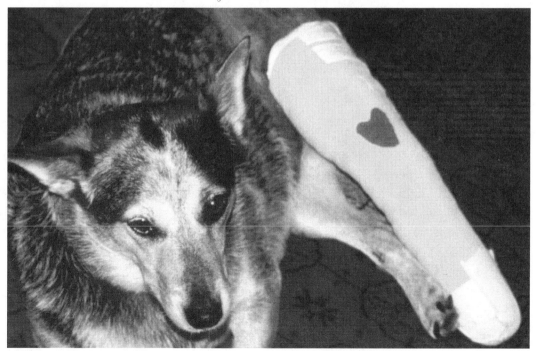

ALASKA

Anchorage - *Anchorage Borough*
Pet Emergency Treatment, Inc.
2320 East Dowling Road
Anchorage, AK 99507
Phone: (907) 274-5636
Fax: (907) 274-5133
Website:
   www.petemergencytreatment.com
Hours: 24 hours a day

Fairbanks -
   Fairbanks North Star Borough
After Hours Veterinary
   Emergency Clinic, Inc.
8 Bonnie Avenue
Fairbanks, AK 99701
Phone: (907) 479-2700
Fax: (907) 479-5195
Website: www.ahveci.com
Hours: Mon -Thurs (6pm-8am);
         Weekends from Fri (6pm) -
         Mon (8am); Holidays

Loretta

ARIZONA

Chandler - *Maricopa County*
First Regional Animal Hospital
1233 West Warner Road
Chandler, AZ 85224
Phone: (480) 732-0018
Fax: (480) 732-0335
Website: www.firstregionalvet.com
Hours: 24 hours a day;
       7 days a week;
       365 days a year
Note: Pet emergency transportation
       may be available.

Flagstaff - *Coconino County*
Canyon Pet Hospital
1054 East Old Canyon Court
Flagstaff, AZ 86001
Phone: (928) 774-5197
Fax: --
Website:
    www.canyonpethospitalaz.com
Hours: Extended with 24-Hour
       Emergency Service in the
       Flagstaff, Williams, and Grand
       Canyon area (also Mobile
       Service to those areas).

Gilbert - *Maricopa County*
Arizona Veterinary Specialists (AVS),
    LLC & The Emergency Animal
    Clinic (EAC), PLC
86 West Juniper Avenue
Gilbert, AZ 85233
Phone: (480) 635-1110 (AVS)
Phone: (480) 497-0222 (EAC)
Fax: (480) 892-0540 (AVS)
Fax: (480) 497-9575 (EAC)
Website: www.azvs.com (includes
    4 locations)
Hours: 24 hours a day;
       7 days a week;
       365 days a year

Mesa - *Maricopa County*
VCA Animal Referral and Emergency
    Center of Arizona (ARECA)
1648 North Country Club Drive
Mesa, AZ 85201
Phone: (480) 898-0001
Fax: (480) 898-3111
Website: www.vcaareca.com
Hours: 24 hours a day;
       7 days a week;
       365 days a year

Peoria - *Maricopa County*
Arizona Veterinary Specialists (AVS),
    LLC & The Emergency Animal
    Clinic (EAC), PLC
9875 West Peoria Avenue
Peoria, AZ 85345
Phone: (623) 974-1520
Fax: (623) 974-7738
Website: www.azvs.com (includes
    4 locations)
Hours: 24 hours a day;
       7 days a week;
       365 days a year

Phoenix - *Maricopa County*
Arizona Veterinary Specialists (AVS),
    LLC & The Emergency Animal
    Clinic (EAC), PLC
2260 West Glendale Avenue
Phoenix, AZ 85021
Phone: (602) 995-3757
Fax: (602) 864-1019
Website: www.azvs.com (includes
    4 locations)
Hours: 24 hours a day;
       7 days a week;
       365 days a year

(Arizona continues)

ARIZONA (continued)

North Valley Animal
   Emergency Center
3134 West Carefree Highway - Suite 2
Phoenix, AZ 85086
Phone: (623) 516-8571
Fax: (623) 516-0035
Website: www.nvanimalemergency.com
Hours: Mon - Fri (6pm-8am);
       Weekends from Sat (noon) -
       Mon (8am); Holidays

Scottsdale - *Maricopa County*
Arizona Veterinary Specialists (AVS),
   LLC & The Emergency Animal
   Clinic (EAC), PLC
14202 North Scottsdale Road - Suite 163
Scottsdale, AZ 85254
Phone: (480) 949-8001
Fax: (480) 481-0036
Website: www.azvs.com (includes
   4 locations)
Hours: 24 hours a day; 7 days a week;
       365 days a year

Paradise Valley Emergency
   Animal Clinic
6969 East Shea Boulevard - Suite 225
Scottsdale, AZ 85254
Phone: (480) 991-1845
Fax: (480) 998-8941
Website: www.vcaparadisevalleyaz.com
Hours: Mon - Thurs (5pm-8am);
       Fri (5pm-midnight);
       Sat & Sun - 24 hours

Mr. Moe

Chuckie Low-Legs

Tucson - *Pima County*
Animal Emergency Service
4832 East Speedway Boulevard
Tucson, AZ 85712
Phone: (520) 326-7449
Fax: (520) 327-4575
Website: --
Hours: 24 hours a day; 7 days a week

Ina Road Animal Hospital
7320 La Cholla Boulevard - Suite 114
Tucson, AZ 85741
Phone: (520) 544-7700
Fax: (520) 297-2694
Website:
   www.inaroadanimalhospital.com
Hours: 18 hours day (7am-1am);
       365 days a year;
       24 hour nursing care

Southern Arizona Veterinary
   Specialty & Emergency Center -
   Central Location
141 East Fort Lowell
Tucson, AZ 85705
Phone: (520) 888-3177
Fax: (520) 888-3725
Website: www.southernazvets.com
Hours: 24 hours a day; 7 days a week;
       365 days a year

Southern Arizona Veterinary
   Specialty & Emergency Center -
   East Side Location
7474 East Broadway Boulevard
Tucson, AZ 85710
Phone: (520) 888-3177
Fax: (520) 886-2436
Website: www.southernazvets.com
Hours: 24 hours a day;
         7 days a week;
         365 days a year

Valley Animal Hospital, P.C.
4984 East 22nd Street
Tucson, AZ 85711
Phone: (520) 748-0331
Fax: (520) 748-0897
Website:
www.tusconvalleyanimalhospital.com
Hours: 24 hours day;
         7 days a week;
         365 days a year
         (always staffed)

Veterinary Specialty Center of Tucson
4909 North La Canada Drive
Tucson, AZ 85704
Phone: (520) 795-9955
Fax: (520) 795-9960
Website: www.vetspecialtytucson.com
Hours: 24 hours a day;
         7 days a week;
         365 days a year

Tater

ARKANSAS

Fort Smith - *Sebastian County*
Fort Smith Animal Emergency
    Clinic (AEC)
4301 Regions Park Drive
Fort Smith, AR 72916
Phone: (479) 649-3100
Fax: (479) 646-3109
Website: www.ftsmithaec.com
Hours: Mon - Thurs (6pm-7am);
        Sat & Sun - 24 hours

Baily (being very good)

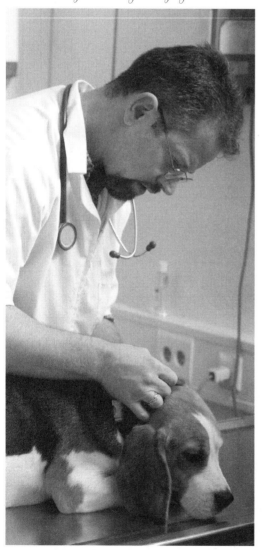

North Little Rock - *Pulaski County*
After Hour Animal Hospital
290 Smokey Lane
North Little Rock, AR 72117
Phone: (501) 955-0911
Fax: (501) 945-6930
Website: --
Hours: Mon - Fri (6pm-7am);
        Weekends from Sat (noon) -
        Mon (7am); Holidays

Animal Emergency & Specialty Clinic
8735 Sheltie Drive
North Little Rock, AR 72113
Phone: (501) 224-3784
Fax: (501) 224-3785
Website: --
Hours: Mon - Fri (6pm-7:30am);
        Weekends from Sat (noon) -
        Mon (7:30am)

Springdale - *Washington County*
Animal Emergency Clinic of
    Northwest Arkansas
1110 Mathias Drive - Suite E
Springdale, AR 72762
Phone: (479) 927-0007
Fax: (479) 927-1458
Website: --
Hours: Mon - Thurs (6pm-7am);
        Weekends from Fri (6pm) to
        Mon (7am)

CALIFORNIA

Anaheim - *Orange County*
Yorba Regional Animal Hospital
8290 East Crystal Drive
Anaheim, CA 92807
Phone: (714) 921-8700
Fax: (714) 283-1262
Website: www.yorbaregionalvets.com
Hours: 24 hours a day
Note: Daytime practice also at
  this location.

Antioch - *Contra Costa County*
East Bay Veterinary Emergency
1312 Sunset Drive
Antioch, CA 94509
Phone: (925) 754-5001
Fax: (925) 754-5005
Website: www.ebve.com
Hours: Mon - Fri (6pm-8am);
  Sat & Sun & Holidays - 24 hrs

Arroyo Grande -
  San Luis Obispo County
Central Coast Pet Emergency
1558 West Branch Street
Arroyo Grande, CA 93420
Phone: (805) 489-6573
Fax: (805) 489-5470
Website: --
Hours: Mon - Thurs (6pm-8am);
  Weekends from Fri (6pm) -
  Mon (8am); Holidays

Atascadero - *San Luis Obispo County*
Atascadero Pet Emergency Center
9575 El Camino Real
Atascadero, CA 93422
Phone: (805) 466-3880
Fax: (805) 466-3830
Website: www.apetcenter.com
Hours: 24 hours a day;
  7 days a week;
  365 days a year

Bakersfield - *Kern County*
Animal Emergency and Urgent Care
4300 Easton Drive - Suite 1
Bakersfield, CA 93309
Phone: (661) 322-6019
Toll Free: (888) 739-4914
Fax: (661) 322-8256
Website: www.ervets.net
Hours: Nights; Weekends; Holidays

Bellflower - *Los Angeles County*
VCA Lakewood Animal Hospital
17801 Lakewood Boulevard
Bellflower, CA 90706
Phone: (562) 633-8126
Fax: (562) 529-2043
Website: www.vcalakewoodca.com
Hours: 24 hours a day;
  7 days a week

(California continues)

Lyle (not lovin' it)

CALIFORNIA (continued)

Berkeley - *Alameda County*
Berkeley Dog & Cat Hospital
2126 Haste Street
Berkeley, CA 94704
Phone: (510) 848-5041
Fax: (510) 548-4071
Website: www.berkeleydogandcat.com
Hours: 24 hours a day; 7 days a week
Note: Regular appointments also
available.

Pet Emergency Treatment Service
1048 University Avenue
Berkeley, CA 94710
Phone: (510) 548-6684
Fax: --
Website: www.berkeleypets.org
Hours: Mon - Fri (6pm-8am);
Weekends from Sat (8am) -
Mon (8am); Holidays

Hoss

Campbell - *Santa Clara County*
United Emergency Animal Clinic -
Campbell Location
911 Dell Avenue
Campbell, CA 95008
Phone: (408) 371-6252
Fax: --
Website:
www.emergencyanimalclinic.com
Hours: Mon - Thurs (6pm-8am);
Weekends from Fri (6pm) -
Mon (8am); Holidays

Capitola - *Santa Cruz County*
Pacific Veterinary Specialists and
Emergency Service
1980 41st Avenue
Capitola, CA 95010
Phone: (831) 476-0667 Emergency
Phone: (831) 476-2584 Specialty
Fax: (831) 476-6729
Website: www.pvses.com
Hours: Mon - Thurs (6pm-8am);
Weekends from Fri (6pm) -
Mon (8am); Holidays
Note: Daytime practice also at
this location.

Chula Vista - *San Diego County*
Pet Emergency & Specialty
Center/South County Hospital
885 Canarios Court - Suite 108
Chula Vista, CA 91910
Phone: (619) 591-4802
Fax: --
Website: www.pescsandiego.com
Hours: Mon - Fri (6pm-8am);
Sat & Sun & Holidays - 24 hrs

South County Animal
Emergency Clinic
(located at Bonita Pet Hospital)
3438 Bonita Road
Chula Vista, CA 91910
Phone: (619) 427-2881 Emergency
Phone: (619) 427-2233 Main Number
Fax: (619) 425-7262
Website: --
Hours: 24 hours a day

I ♥ Himalayans

Concord - *Contra Costa County*
Contra Costa Veterinary
    Emergency Center
1410 Monument Boulevard
Concord, CA 94520
Phone: (925) 798-2900
Fax: (925) 798-4982
Website: www.ccvec.com
Hours: 24 hours a day; 7 days a week

Corona - *Riverside County*
Aacacia Animal Hospital
939 West Sixth Street
Corona, CA 92879
Phone: (951) 371-1002
Fax: --
Website: www.coronapethospital.com
Hours: 24 hours a day; 7 days a week

Culver City - *Los Angeles County*
Advanced Critical Care and
    Internal Medicine (ACC&IM)
9599 Jefferson Boulevard
Culver City, CA 90232
Phone: (310) 558-6100
Fax: (310) 558-6199
Website: www.accim.net
Hours: 24 hours a day; 7 days a week

DAVIS - *Yolo County*
University of California - Davis
School of Veterinary Medicine
William R. Pritchard Veterinary
    Medical Teaching Hospital
Davis, CA 95616
Phone: (530) 752-1393 Appointments
Phone: (530) 752-0186 Emergency
Fax: (530) 752-9620
Website: www.vetmed.ucdavis.edu
Hours: Emergency Service Available
            24 hours a day;
            365 days a year

Diamond Bar - *Los Angeles County*
East Valley Emergency Pet Clinic, Inc.
938 North Diamond Bar Boulevard
Diamond Bar, CA 91765
Phone: (909) 861-5737
Fax: (909) 861-3286
Website: --
Hours: Mon - Fri (6pm-8am);
            Weekends from Sat (noon) -
            Mon (8am); Holidays

Dublin - *Alameda County*
VETcare Veterinary Emergency &
    Specialist Care Center
7660 Amador Valley Boulevard
Dublin, CA 94568
Phone: (925) 556-1234
Fax: (925) 556-1299
Website: www.emergencyvetcare.com
Hours: 24 hours a day

(California continues)

Charlie

CALIFORNIA (continued)

El Monte - *Los Angeles County*
Emergency Pet Clinic
3254 Santa Anita Avenue
El Monte, CA 91733
Phone: (626) 579-4550
Fax: --
Website: --
Hours: Mon - Fri (6pm-8am);
       Weekends from Sat (noon) -
       Mon (8am); Holidays

Miss Mimi

Encinitas - *San Diego County*
VCA North Coast Veterinary &
   Emergency
414 Encinitas Boulevard
Encinitas, CA 92024
Phone: (760) 632-1072
Fax: (760) 632-0486
Website: www.vcanorthcoast.com
Hours: 24 hours a day;
       7 days a week

Escondido - *San Diego County*
Animal Urgent Care of Escondido
   (formerly Escondido Veterinary
   Urgent Care)
2430-A South Escondido Boulevard
Escondido, CA 92025
Phone: (760) 738-9600
Fax: (760) 738-5204
Website: www.animalurgentcare.com
Hours: 24 hours a day;
       7 days a week;
       365 days a year

Fair Oaks - *Sacramento County*
Associated Veterinary Emergency
   Service or Greenback Vet Hospital
8311 Greenback Lane
Fair Oaks, CA 95628
Phone: (916) 725-1711
Fax: (916) 725-4584
Website: --
Hours: 24 hours a day

Fairfield - *Solano County*
Solano-Napa Pet Emergency Clinic
4437 Central Place - Suite B3
Fairfield, CA 94534
Phone: (707) 864-1444 Regular Office
Phone: (707) 554-6311 Emergency
Fax: --
Website: www.solanopetemergency.com
Hours: Mon - Fri (6pm-8am);
       Sat & Sun & Holidays - 24 hrs

Fountain Valley - *Orange County*
VCA All Care Animal Referral Center
18440 Amistad Street - Suite E
Fountain Valley, CA 92708
Phone: (714) 963-0909
Fax: (714) 964-7007
Website: www.vcaacarc.com
Hours: 24 hours a day;
       7 days a week

Fremont - *Alameda County*
Ohlone Veterinary
   Emergency Clinic, Inc.
1618 Washington Boulevard
Fremont, CA 94539
Phone: (510) 657-6620
Fax: (510) 657-6204
Website:
   www.ohlonevetemergencyclinic.com
Hours: Mon - Fri (6pm-8am);
       Sat & Sun & Holidays - 24 hrs

Fresno - *Fresno County*
Fresno Pet Emergency &
   Referral Center, Inc.
7375 North Palm Bluffs Avenue
Fresno, CA 93711
Phone: (559) 437-3766
Fax: (559) 437-0222
Website: www.fresnopeter.com
Hours: 24 hours a day;
       7 days a week

Veterinary Emergency Service
1639 North Fresno Street
Fresno, CA 93703
Phone: (559) 486-0520
Fax: --
Website: www.vesfresno.com
Hours: 24 hours a day;
       7 days a week

Garden Grove - *Orange County*
Orange County Emergency
   Pet Clinic
12750 Garden Grove Boulevard
Garden Grove, CA 92843
Phone: (714) 537-3032
Fax: (714) 539-0815
Website: www.er4yourpet.com
Hours: Mon - Fri (6pm-8am);
       Weekends from Sat (noon) -
       Mon (8am); Holidays
Note: Pet emergency transportation
       may be available.

Granada Hills - *Los Angeles County*
Chatoak Pet Clinic
17659 Chatsworth Street
Granada Hills, CA 91344
Phone: (818) 363-7444
Fax: (818) 363-1605
Website: www.pmc-chatoak.com
Hours: 24 hours a day

Grand Terrace - *San Bernardino County*
Animal Emergency Clinic
12022 LaCrosse Avenue
Grand Terrace, CA 92313
Phone: (909) 825-9350
Fax: (909) 783-6820
Website: --
Hours: Mon - Fri (6pm-8am);
       Sat & Sun & Holidays - 24 hrs

La Habra - *Orange County*
Orange County Emergency Pet Clinic
1474 South Harbor Boulevard
La Habra, CA 90631
Phone: (714) 441-2925 or
   (562) 690-2925
Fax: (714) 441-0538
Website: www.er4yourpet.com
Hours: Mon - Fri (6pm-8am);
       Weekends from Sat (noon) -
       Mon (8am); Holidays
Note: Pet emergency transportation
       may be available.

(California continues)

Dodger Dog

CALIFORNIA (continued)

La Mesa - *San Diego County*
Pet Emergency & Specialty Center/
  La Mesa Hospital
Jackson Square Center
5232 Jackson Drive - Suite 105
La Mesa, CA 91941
Phone: (619) 462-4800
Fax: (619) 462-7224
Website: www.pescsandiego.com
Hours: 24 hours a day;
       7 days a week;
       365 days a year

Laguna Niguel - *Orange County*
Crown Valley Animal Care Center
28892 Crown Valley Parkway
Laguna Niguel, CA 92677
Phone: (949) 495-1123
Fax: --
Website:
  www.animal-care-centers.com
Hours: 24 hours a day; 7 days a week

Bandit ("it's time for a walk")

Lancaster - *Los Angeles County*
Animal Emergency Clinic
1055 West Avenue - Suite 101
  (also known as Columbia Way)
Lancaster, CA 93534
Phone: (661) 723-3959
Fax: --
Website: www.animalemergencyclinic.org
Hours: Mon - Fri (6pm-8am);
       Weekends from Sat (noon) -
       Mon (8am); Holidays

Lawndale - *Los Angeles County*
Advanced Veterinary Care Center
15926 Hawthorne Boulevard
Lawndale, CA 90260
Phone: (310) 542-8018
Fax: (310) 542-8098
Website:
www.advancedveterinarycarecenter.com
Hours: 24 hours a day; 7 days a week
Note: Regular appointments
      also available.

Los Altos - *Santa Clara County*
Adobe Animal Hospital
396 First Street
Los Altos, CA 94022
Phone: (650) 948-9661
Fax: (650) 948-1465
Website: www.adobe-animal.com
Hours: 24 hours a day; 7 days a week;
      365 days a year

Los Angeles - *Los Angeles County*
Animal Specialty Group
4641 Colorado Boulevard
Los Angeles, CA 90039
Phone: (818) 244-7977
Fax: (818) 507-9418
Website: www.asgvets.com
Hours: Mon - Fri (2pm-8am);
      Weekends 24 hours

Animal Surgical and Emergency Center
1535 South Sepulveda Boulevard
Los Angeles, CA 90025
Phone: (310) 473-1561
Fax: (310) 479-8976
Website: www.asecvets.com
Hours: 24 hours a day;
      7 days a week;
      365 days a year

California Animal Hospital
1736 South Sepulveda Boulevard
Los Angeles, CA 90025
Phone: (310) 479-3336
Fax: (310) 479-1621
Website: www.californiaanimal.org
Hours: 24 hours a day;
      7 days a week

Eagle Rock Emergency Pet Clinic, Inc.
4254 Eagle Rock Boulevard
Los Angeles, CA 90065
Phone: (323) 254-7382
Fax: (323) 254-1837
Website: --
Hours: Mon - Fri (6pm-8am);
      Weekends from Sat (noon) -
      Mon (8am); Holidays

Benny

VCA West Los Angeles Animal Hospital
1818 South Sepulveda Boulevard
Los Angeles, CA 90025
Phone: (310) 473-2951
Fax: (310) 472-2779
Website: www.vcawla.com
Hours: 24 hours a day; 7 days a week

Mission Viejo - *Orange County*
Animal Urgent Care of
   South Orange County
28085 Hillcrest
Mission Viejo, CA 92692
Phone: (949) 364-6228
Fax: (949) 364-1730
Website: --
Hours: Mon - Fri (6pm-8am);
      Weekends from Sat (noon) -
      Mon (8am); Holidays

Modesto - *Stanislaus County*
Veterinary Emergency Clinic
1800 Prescott Road - Suite E
Modesto, CA 95350
Phone: (209) 527-8844
Fax: (209) 527-8816
Website: www.vetemergencyclinic.com
Hours: Mon - Fri (6pm-8am);
      Weekends from Sat (noon) -
      Mon (8am); Holidays

Monterey - *Monterey County*
Monterey Peninsula Veterinary
   Emergency & Specialty Center
20 Lower Ragsdale Drive - Suite 150
Monterey, CA 93940
Phone: (831) 373-7374
Fax: (831) 373-4482
Website: www.mpvesc.com
Hours: 24 hours a day;
      7 days a week

(California continues)

CALIFORNIA (continued)

Murrieta - *Riverside County*
California Veterinary Specialists
   Murrieta Hospital Location
25100 Hancock Avenue - Suite 116
Murrieta, CA 92562
Phone: (951) 600-9803
Fax: (951) 600-7758
Website:
www.californiaveterinaryspecialists.com
Hours: 24 hours a day; 7 days a week;
      365 days a year

Newhall - *Los Angeles County*
All Creatures Emergency Center
22722 Lyons Avenue - Suite 5
Newhall, CA 91321
Phone: (661) 291-1121
Fax: (661) 291-1166
Website:
   www.all-creatures-emergency.com
Hours: Mon - Fri (6pm-8am);
      Sat & Sun & Holidays - 24 hrs

Newport Beach - *Orange County*
Central Orange County Emergency
   Animal Clinic
3720 Campus Drive - Suite D
Newport Beach, CA 92660
Phone: (949) 261-7979
Fax: --
Website: --
Hours: Mon - Fri (6pm-8am);
      Weekends from Sat (noon) -
      Mon (8am); Holidays

Norwalk - *Los Angeles County*
Crossroads Animal Emergency &
   Referral Center
11057 East Rosecrans Avenue
Norwalk, CA 90650
Phone: (562) 863-2522
Toll Free: (800) 345-9088
Fax: (562) 863-0643
Website:
www.crossroadsanimalemergency.com
Hours: Mon - Fri (6pm-8am);
      Weekends from Sat (4pm) -
      Mon (8am); Holidays

Pasadena - *Los Angeles County*
Animal Emergency Clinic
2121 East Foothill Boulevard
Pasadena, CA 91107
Phone: (626) 564-0704
Toll Free: (866) 738-3937 or
      (800) PET-3911
Website: --
Hours: Mon - Fri (6pm-8am);
      Weekends from Sat (noon) -
      Mon (8am); Holidays

Poway - *San Diego County*
Animal Emergency Clinic
12775 Poway Road
Poway, CA 92064
Phone: (858) 748-7387
Fax: (858) 748-6438
Website: www.animalemergencysd.com
Hours: Mon - Thurs (6pm-8am);
      Weekends from Fri (6pm) -
      Mon (8am); Holidays

Reseda - *Los Angeles County*
McClave Veterinary Hospital
6950 Reseda Boulevard
Reseda, CA 91335
Phone: (818) 881-5102
Fax: (818) 881-2831
Website: www.mcclavevethospital.com
Hours: 24 hours a day; 7 days a week
Note: Daytime practice also at
this location.

Rohnert Park - *Sonoma County*
Animal Care Center
6470 Redwood Drive
Rohnert Park, CA 94928
Phone: (707) 584-4343
Fax: (707) 586-9042
Website: www.accsonoma.com
Hours: 24 hours a day; 7 days a week;
365 days a year

Sacramento - *Sacramento County*
Mueller Pet Medical Center, Inc.
6420 Freeport Boulevard
Sacramento, CA 95822
Phone: (916) 428-9202
Fax: (916) 428-9206
Website:
www.muelleranimalhospital.com
Hours: 24 hours a day; 7 days a week;
365 days a year

Sacramento Emergency
Veterinary Clinic
2201 El Camino Avenue - Suite A
Sacramento, CA 95821
Phone: (916) 922-3425
Fax: (916) 922-0219
Website:
www.sacemergencyvetclinic.com
Hours: Mon - Fri (6pm-8am);
Sat & Sun & Holidays - 24 hrs

San Diego - *San Diego County*
Animal ER of San Diego
5610 Kearny Mesa Road
San Diego, CA 92111
Phone: (858) 569-0600
Fax: --
Website: --
Hours: Mon - Fri (6pm-8am);
Sat & Sun & Holidays - 24 hrs

VCA Emergency Animal Hospital &
Referral Center
2317 Hotel Circle South
San Diego, CA 92108
Phone: (619) 299-2400
Fax: (619) 299-9068
Website: www.vcaemergency.com
Hours: 24 hours a day; 7 days a week

Veterinary Specialty Hospital
10435 Sorrento Valley Road
San Diego, CA 92121
Phone: (858) 875-7500 Main Number
Phone: (858) 875-7570 Emergency
Fax: --
Website: www.vshsd.com
Hours: 24 hours a day; 7 days a week

(California continues)

Buster

CALIFORNIA (continued)

San Francisco - *San Francisco County*
All Animals Emergency Hospital
1333 Ninth Avenue
San Francisco, CA 94122
Phone: (415) 566-0531
Fax: (415) 566-0989
Website: --
Hours: Mon - Fri (6pm-8am);
    Sat & Sun & Holidays - 24 hrs

Pets Unlimited
2343 Fillmore Street
San Francisco, CA 94115
Phone: (415) 563-6700
Fax: (415) 775-2573
Website: www.petsunlimited.org
Hours: 24 hours a day

San Francisco Veterinary Specialists
    Portrero Hills/Mission District
600 Alabama Street
San Francisco, CA 94110
Phone: (415) 401-9200
Fax: (415) 401-9201
Website: www.sfvs.net
Hours: 24 hours a day; 7 days a week

Honk if you ♥ Great Danes

San Jose - *Santa Clara County*
Emergency Animal Clinic of
    South San Jose - San Jose Location
5440 Thornwood Drive
San Jose, CA 95123
Phone: (408) 578-5622
Fax: --
Website:
    www.emergencyanimalclinic.com
Hours: Mon - Thurs (6pm-8am);
    Weekends from Fri (6pm) -
    Mon (8am); Holidays

San Leandro - *Alameda County*
Bay Area Veterinary Specialists (BAVS)
14790 Washington Avenue
San Leandro, CA 94578
Phone: (510) 483-7387 (PETS)
Fax: (510) 483-7389
Website: www.bayvetspecialists.com
Hours: 24 hours a day

San Marcos - *San Diego County*
California Veterinary Specialists
100 North Rancho Santa Fe Road -
    Suite 133
San Marcos, CA 92069
Phone: (760) 734-4433
Fax: (760) 734-6523
Website:
www.californiaveterinaryspecialists.com
Hours: 24 hours a day

San Mateo - *San Mateo County*
Northern Peninsula Veterinary
    Emergency Clinic
227 Amphlett Boulevard
San Mateo, CA 94401
Phone: (650) 348-2575
Fax: --
Website: --
Hours: Mon - Fri (5:30pm-8am);
    Sat & Sun & Holidays - 24 hrs

San Rafael - *Marin County*
Pet Emergency & Specialty Center
    of Marin
901 East Francisco Boulevard
San Rafael, CA 94901
Phone: (415) 456-7372
Fax: (415) 457-6318
Website: www.petemergencycenter.com
Hours: 24 hours a day;
    7 days a week;
    365 days a year

Santa Barbara - *Santa Barbara County*
CARE Hospital - California Animal
   Referral & Emergency Hospital
301 East Haley Street
Santa Barbara, CA 93101
Phone: (805) 899-CARE (2273)
Fax: (805) 965-0070
Website: www.carehospital.org
Hours: 24 hours a day;
      7 days a week;
      365 days a year

Pacific Emergency Pet Hospital
2963 State Street
Santa Barbara, CA 93199
Phone: (805) 682-5120
Fax: --
Websites: www.sbwave.com/peph/ or
   www.pacificemergencypethosp.com
Hours: Mon - Fri (6pm-8am);
      Sat & Sun & Holidays - 24 hrs

Santa Cruz - *Santa Cruz County*
Santa Cruz Veterinary Hospital
2585 Soquel Drive
Santa Cruz, CA 95065
Phone: (831) 475-5400
Fax: --
Website:
www.santacruzveterinaryhospital.com
Hours: 24 hours a day;
      7 days a week

Santa Monica - *Los Angeles County*
Westside Animal Emergency Hospital
1304 Wilshire Boulevard
Santa Monica, CA 90403
Phone: (310) 451-8962
Fax: --
Website: --
Hours: Tues - Sat (6pm-8am);
      Call for other hours.

Santa Rosa - *Sonoma County*
Emergency Animal Hospital of
   Santa Rosa (located at Redwood
   Veterinary Clinic)
1946 Santa Rosa Avenue
Santa Rosa, CA 95407
Phone: (707) 542-4012
Fax: (707) 542-2440
Website: www.redwoodvetclinic.com
Hours: 24 hours a day; 7 days a week
Note: Daytime practice also at
      this location.

PetCare Veterinary Hospital
1370 Fulton Road
Santa Rosa, CA 95401
Phone: (707) 579-5900
Fax: (707) 579-9512
Website: www.pcvh.com
Hours: 24 hours a day; 7 days a week

Mona

Sherman Oaks - *Los Angeles County*
Beverly Oaks Animal Hospital
14302 Ventura Boulevard
Sherman Oaks, CA 91423
Phone: (818) 788-2022
Fax: --
Website: www.beverlyoaks.org
Hours: 24 hours a day

(California continues)

CALIFORNIA (continued)

Shingle Springs - *El Dorado County*
Mother Lode Pet Emergency Clinic
4050 Durock Road
Shingle Springs, CA 95682
Phone 1: (530) 676-9044
Phone 2: (916) 358-5455
Fax: --
Website: www.motherlodepec.com
Hours: Mon - Fri (6pm-8am);
        Weekends from Sat (8am) -
        Mon (8am)

Peaches

South Pasadena - *Los Angeles County*
TLC Pet Medical Centers
1412 Huntington Drive
South Pasadena, CA 91030
Phone: (626) 441-8555
Fax: (626) 441-8525
Website: www.tlcvet.com
Hours: 24 hours a day;
        7 days a week;
        365 days a year

Studio City - *Los Angeles County*
Animal Emergency Centre
11730 Ventura Boulevard
Studio City, CA 91604
Phone: (818) 760-3882
Fax: --
Website: www.valleypet911.com
Hours: Mon - Thurs (6pm-8am);
        Weekends from Fri (6pm) -
        Mon (8am); Holidays

Temecula - *Riverside County*
Emergency Pet Clinic
27443 Jefferson Avenue
Temecula, CA 92590
Phone: (951) 695-5044
Fax: --
Website: --
Hours: Weeknights (6pm-8am);
        Weekends & Major Holidays -
        24 hours

Thousand Oaks - *Ventura County*
Pet Emergency Clinic, Inc.
2967 North Moorpark Road
Thousand Oaks, CA 91360
Phone: (805) 492-2436
Fax: (805) 642-4898
Website: www.petemergencyclinic.com
Hours: Mon - Fri (6pm-8am);
        Sat & Sun & Holidays - 24 hrs

Thousand Palms - *Riverside County*
Animal Emergency Clinic of the Desert
72-374 Ramon Road
Thousand Palms, CA 92276
Phone: (760) 343-3438
Fax: --
Website: www.animaler1000palms.com
Hours: Mon - Fri (5pm-8am);
        Weekends from Sat (noon) -
        Mon (8am); Holidays

Torrance - *Los Angeles County*
Animal Emergency Referral Center
3511 Pacific Coast Highway - Suite A
Torrance, CA 90505
Phone: (310) 325-3000
Fax: (310) 257-0900
Website:
    www.animalemergencyreferral.com
Hours: 24 hours a day;
        7 days a week

Emergency Pet Clinic of South Bay
2325 Torrance Boulevard
Torrance, CA 90501
Phone: (310) 320-8300
Fax: --
Website: www.emergencypets.com
Hours: Mon - Fri (6pm-8am);
Weekends from Sat (noon) -
Mon (8am); Holidays

Tustin - *Orange County*
Advanced Critical Care &
Internal Medicine (ACC&IM)
2965 & 3021 Edinger Avenue
Tustin, CA 92780
Phone: (949) 654-8950
Fax: (949) 936-0079
Website: www.accim.net
Hours: 24 hours a day;
7 days a week

Upland - *San Bernardino County*
Inland Valley Emergency
10 West 7th Street
Upland, CA 91786
Phone: (909) 931-7871
Toll Free: (877) 973-8911
Fax: --
Website: --
Hours: Mon - Fri (6pm-8am);
Weekends from Sat (noon) -
Mon (8am); Holidays

VCA Central Animal Hospital
281 North Central Avenue
Upland, CA 91786
Phone: (909) 981-2855
Fax: (909) 985-9398
Website: www.vcacentral.com
Hours: 24 hours a day;
7 days a week;
365 days a year

Vallejo - *Solano County*
Solano-Napa Pet Emergency Clinic
4437 Central Place - Suite B3
Vallejo, CA 94534
Phone 1: (707) 554-6311
Phone 2: (707) 864-1444
Fax: --
Website: www.solanopetemergency.com
Hours: Mon - Fri (6pm-8am);
Sat & Sun & Holidays - 24 hrs
Note: Daytime practice also at
this location.

Ventura - *Ventura County*
Pet Emergency Clinic, Inc.
2301 South Victoria Avenue
Ventura, CA 93003
Phone: (805) 642-8562
Fax: (805) 642-4898
Website: www.petemergencyclinic.com
Hours: Mon - Fri (6pm-8am);
Weekends from Sat (8am) -
Mon (8am); Holidays

(California continues)

Bella

CALIFORNIA (continued)

Victorville - *San Bernardino County*
Animal Emergency Clinic
15532 Bear Valley Road
Victorville, CA 92395
Phone: (760) 962-1122
Fax: --
Website: --
Hours: Mon - Fri (6pm-8am);
     Weekends from Sat (noon) -
     Mon (8am); Holidays

Visalia - *Tulare County*
Tulare-Kings Veterinary
   Emergency Services
4946 West Mineral King
Visalia, CA 93278
Phone: (559) 739-7054
Fax: --
Website: --
Hours: Daily 5pm to 8am the
     following day

Vista - *San Diego County*
Coastal Emergency Animal Hospital
1900 Hacienda Drive
Vista, CA 92083
Phone: (760) 630-6343
Fax: --
Website: --
Hours: Mon - Fri (5pm-8am);
     Sat & Sun & Holidays - 24 hrs

West Hollywood - *Los Angeles County*
TLC Pet Medical Centers
   West Hollywood
8725 Santa Monica Boulevard
West Hollywood, CA 90069
Phone: (310) 859-4852
Fax: (310) 289-8552
Websites: www.tlcvet.com
Hours: 24 hours a day;
     7 days a week

Woodland Hills - *Los Angeles County*
Animal Emergency Care Center
20051-D Ventura Boulevard
Woodland Hills, CA 91364
Phone: (818) 887-2262
Fax: (818) 704-0323
Website:
 www.animalemergencycarecenter.com
Hours: Mon - Thurs (6pm-8am);
     Weekends from Fri (6pm) -
     Mon (8am); Holidays

COLORADO

Aurora - *Adams County*
Aurora Veterinary Emergency Center
18511 East Hampden Avenue
Aurora, CO 80013
Phone: (303) 699-1665
Fax: --
Website: --
Hours: Weeknights (6pm-8am);
  Weekends - 24 hours

Basalt - *Eagle County*
Valley Emergency Pet Care
180 Fiou Lane - Suite 101
Basalt, CO 81621
Phone: (970) 927-5066
Fax: (970) 927-5064
Website: --
Hours: Mon - Fri (5pm-8am);
  Sat & Sun & Holidays - 24 hrs

Boulder - *Boulder County*
VCA All Pets Animal Hospital Boulder
5290 Manhattan Circle
Boulder, CO 80303
Telephone: (303) 499-5335
Fax: (303) 499-5362
Website: www.vcaallpetsboulder.com
Hours: 24 hours a day;
  7 days a week

Wheat Ridge Animal Hospital Boulder
  - Boulder Location (previously
  Boulder Emergency Pet Clinic)
1658 30th Street
Boulder, CO 80301
Phone: (720) 974-5802
Fax: (303) 440-0649
Website: www.wrah.com
Hours: 24 hours a day; 7 days a week;
  365 days a year

Broomfield - *Broomfield County*
Animal Emergency & Referral Center
1480 West Midway Boulevard
Broomfield, CO 80020
Phone: (303) 464-7744
Fax: (303) 460-7565
Website: www.aercbroomfield.com
Hours: Weeknights (6pm-8am);
  Weekends & Holidays - 24 hrs

Colorado Springs - *El Paso County*
Animal Emergency Care Center North
5752 North Academy Boulevard
Colorado Springs, CO 80918
Phone: (719) 260-7141
Fax: (719) 260-0823
Website: --
Hours: Mon - Thurs (6pm-8am);
  Weekends & Holidays - 24 hrs

(Colorado continues)

Mr. Big

COLORADO (continued)

Animal Emergency Care Center South
3775 Airport Road
Colorado Springs, CO 80910
Phone: (719) 578-9300
Fax: (719) 578-0881
Website: --
Hours: Mon - Thurs (6pm-8am);
     Weekends from Fri (6pm) -
     Mon (8am); Holidays

Emergency and Critical Care
  Pet Hospital
5956 Stetson Hills Boulevard
Colorado Springs, CO 80922
Phone: (719) 473-0482
Fax: --
Website: --
Hours: Mon - Fri (5:30pm-9am);
     Weekends from Sat (noon) -
     Mon (9am)

Denver - *Denver County*
Alameda East Veterinary Hospital
9770 East Alameda Avenue
Denver, CO 80247
Phone: (303) 366-2639
Fax: (303) 344-8150
Website: www.alamedaeast.com
Hours: 24 hours a day;
     7 days a week;
     365 days a year

Northside Emergency Pet Clinic, P.C.
945 West 124th Avenue
Denver, CO 80234
Phone: (303) 252-7722
Fax: --
Website: www.emergencypetclinics.com
Hours: Mon - Fri (5:30pm-8am);
     Sat & Sun & Holidays - 24 hrs

Englewood - *Arapahoe County*
Veterinary Referral Center of Colorado
3550 South Jason Street
Englewood, CO 80110
Phone: (303) 874-7387
Fax: --
Website: www.vrcc.com
Hours: Mon - Fri (4pm-8am);
     Sat & Sun & Holidays - 24 hrs
Note: Daytime practice also at
     this location.

Evans - *Weld County*
Pets Emergency Treatment Services
3629 23rd Avenue
Evans, CO 80620
Phone: (970) 339-8700
Fax: (970) 339-3944
Website: www.petsemergency.com
Hours: Mon - Fri (6pm-8am);
     Sat & Sun & Holidays - 24 hrs

Shadow and Howie

FORT COLLINS - *Larimer County*
Colorado State University
College of Veterinary Medicine &
    Biomedical Sciences; Emergency
    and Critical Care Medicine
West Drake Road
Fort Collins, CO 80523
Emergency Phone: (970) 221-4535
Website: www.cvmbs.colostate.edu
Hours: 24 hours a day;
        7 days a week;
        365 days a year

Tinker

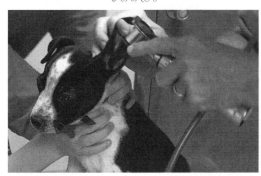

Fort Collins - *Larimer County*
Veterinary Emergency Hospital
816 South Lemay Avenue
Fort Collins, CO 80524
Phone: (970) 484-8080
Fax: (970) 484-8111
Website: --
Hours: Mon - Fri (6pm-8am);
        Sat & Sun & Holidays - 24 hrs

Grand Junction - *Mesa County*
Veterinary Emergency Center
1660 North Avenue
Grand Junction, CO 81501
Phone: (970) 255-1911
Fax: (970) 255-9919
Website:
  www.veterinaryemergencycenter.com
Hours: Mon - Fri (6pm-8am);
        Sat & Sun & Holidays - 24 hrs

Highlands Ranch - *Douglas County*
Animal Hospital Center Emergency &
    Critical Care
5640 County Line Place - Suite One
Highlands Ranch, CO 80126
Phone: (303) 740-9595
Fax: (303) 740-9569
Website: www.animalhospitalcenter.com
Hours: 24 hours a day;
        7 days a week;
        365 days a year

Lakewood - *Jefferson County*
ACCESS/Animal Critical Care &
    Emergency Services
1597 Wadsworth Boulevard
Lakewood, CO 80214
Phone: (303) 239-1200
Fax: --
Website: --
Hours: 24 hours a day; 7 days a week

Littleton - *Arapahoe County*
Animal ER
221 West County Line Road
Littleton, CO 80129
Phone: (720) 283-9348
Fax: --
Website:
www.coloradoveterinaryspecialists.com
Hours: Mon - Fri (6pm-8am);
        Sat & Sun & Holidays - 24 hrs
Note: Daytime practice is located at
        223 West County Line Road.

(Colorado continues)

Bun-Bun

COLORADO (continued)

Columbine Animal Hospital &
  24 Hour Emergency Clinic
5546 West Canyon Trail
Littleton, CO 80128
Phone: (303) 979-4040
Fax: --
Website: www.columbineanimal.com
Hours: 24 hours a day
Note: Regular appointments
  also available.

Longmont - *Boulder County*
Animal Emergency Center
  of Longmont
230 South Main Street
Longmont, CO 80501
Phone: (303) 678-8844
Toll Free: (888) 712-8844
Fax: (303) 678-8855
Website:
  www.animalemergencycenter.net
Hours: Mon - Fri (6pm-8am);
  Sat & Sun & Holidays - 24 hrs

Loveland - *Larimer County*
Animal Emergency Services of
  Northern Colorado (located at
  Veterinary Specialists of
  Northern Colorado)
201 West 67th Court
Loveland, CO 80538
Phone: (970) 278-0668
Fax: (970) 663-6273
Website: www.vcavsnc.com
Hours: Mon - Fri (6pm-8am);
  Sat & Sun & Holidays - 24 hrs
Note: Daytime practice also at
  this location.

Parker - Douglas *County*
Animal Emergency & Specialty Center
17701 Cottonwood Drive
Parker, CO 80134
Phone: (720) 842-5050
Fax: (720) 842-5060
Website: www.aescparker.com
Hours: 24 hours a day; 7 days a week

Pork Chop

Thornton - *Adams County*
Community Pet Hospital
12311 North Washington Street
Thornton, CO 80241
Phone: (303) 451-1333
Fax: --
Website:
    www.communitypethospital.com
Hours: 24 hours a day
Note: Regular appointments
            also available.

Westminster - *Adams County*
Wheat Ridge Animal Hospital -
    Westminster Location
945 West 124th Avenue
Westminster, CO 80234
Phone: (303) 350-4733
Fax: (303) 350-4734
Website: www.wrah.com
Hours: 24 hours a day;
            7 days a week;
            365 days a year

Wheat Ridge - *Jefferson County*
Wheat Ridge Animal Hospital -
    Wheat Ridge Location
3695 Kipling Street
Wheat Ridge, CO 80033
Phone: (303) 424-3325
Fax: (303) 420-8360
Website: www.wrah.com
Hours: 24 hours a day;
            7 days a week;
            365 days a year

Clementine

CONNECTICUT

Bolton - *Tolland County*
East of the River Veterinary
   Emergency Clinic (located at
   Bolton Veterinary Clinic, P.C.)
222 Boston Turnpike
Bolton, CT 06043
Phone 1: (860) 646-6134
Phone 2: (860) 456-4298
Fax: (860) 643-0418
Website: www.boltonvet.com
Hours: Mon - Fri (6pm-8am);
       Weekends Sat (1pm) -
       Mon (8am); Holidays
Note: Daytime practice also at
       this location.

Cheshire - *New Haven County*
Cheshire Animal Hospital
1572 South Main Street
Cheshire, CT 06410
Phone: (203) 272-3266 Emergency
Fax: (203) 272-2630
Website: www.vcacheshire.com
Hours: 24 hours a day; 7 days a week

Barkley

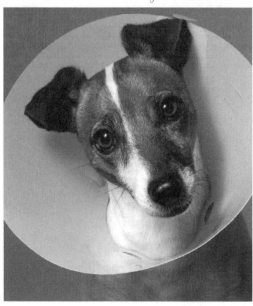

Danbury - *Fairfield County*
Animal Emergency Clinic of Danbury
22 Newtown Road
Danbury, CT 06810
Phone: (203) 790-6383
Fax: --
Website: --
Hours: Mon - Fri (6pm-8am);
       Weekends from Sat (1pm) -
       Mon (8am); Holidays

Farmington - *Hartford County*
Farmington Valley Veterinary
   Emergency Hospital
9 Avonwood Road
Avon, CT 06001
Phone: (860) 674-1886
Fax: (860) 674-8314
Website:
   www.farmingtonemergencyvet.com
Hours: Tues - Thurs (5:30pm-8am);
       Weekends from Fri (5:30pm)
       - Tues (8am)

New Haven - *New Haven County*
New Haven Central Hospital for
   Veterinary Medicine
843 State Street
New Haven, CT 06511
Phone: (203) 865-0878
Fax: (203) 867-5195
Website: www.centralpetvet.com
Hours: 24 hours a day; 7 days a week

Norwalk - *Fairfield County*
Veterinary Referral and
   Emergency Center
123 West Cedar Street
Norwalk, CT 06854
Phone: (203) 854-9960
Fax: (203) 838-5956
Website: www.animaleyeclinic.net
Hours: 24 hours a day
Note: Animal Eye Clinic is also
       located here.

Oakdale-Montville - *New London County*
V-E-T-S (Veterinary Emergency Treatment Services)
8 Enterprise Lane
Oakdale, CT 06370
Phone: (860) 444-8870
Fax: --
Website: www.v-e-t-s.com
Hours: Weeknights (5:30pm - 8:30am); Weekends & Holidays - 24 hrs

Rocky Hill - *Hartford County*
Animal Emergency Hospital of Central Connecticut
588 Cromwell Avenue
Rocky Hill, CT 06067
Phone: (860) 563-4447
Fax: (860) 257-1745
Website: --
Hours: Mon - Fri (5:30pm-8am); Weekends from Sat (1pm) - Mon (8am); Holidays
Note: Daytime practice also at this location.

Polly

Shelton - *Fairfield County*
Shoreline Veterinary Referral & Emergency Center
895 Bridgeport Avenue
Shelton, CT 06484
Phone: (203) 929-8600
Fax: (203) 944-9754
Website: --
Hours: 24 hours a day; 7 days a week

West Hartford - *Hartford County*
Animal Emergency Care Clinic of Hartford County
41 Prospect Avenue
West Hartford, CT 06106
Phone: (860) 233-8387
Fax: --
Website: --
Hours: Mon - Fri (6pm-7:30am); Weekends from Sat (noon) - Mon (7:30am)

Connecticut Veterinary Center, Inc.
470 Oakwood Avenue
West Hartford, CT 06110
Phone: (860) 233-8564
Fax: (860) 233-3206
Website: www.ctvetcenter.com
Hours: 24 hours a day; 7 days a week; 365 days a year

DELAWARE

Dover - *Kent County*
Delmarva Animal Emergency Center
1482 East Lebanon Road
Dover, DE 19901
Phone: (302) 697-0850
Fax: (302) 697-0989
Website: --
Hours: 7 days a week (6pm to 8am)

Newark - *New Castle County*
VCA Newark Animal Hospital
1360 Marrows Road
Newark, DE 19711
Phone: (302) 737-8100
Fax: (302) 737-3843
Website: www.vcanewark.com
Hours: 24 hours a day

The Chipster

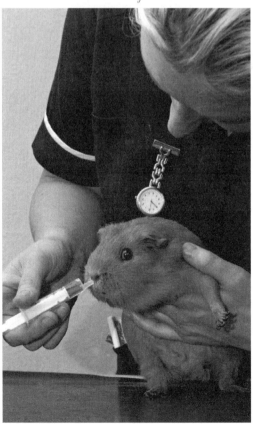

Wilmington - *New Castle County*
Mid-Atlantic Critical Care and
    Emergency Veterinary Center
    (located at Windcrest Animal
    Hospital)
3705 Lancaster Pike
Wilmington, DE 19805
Phone: (302) 998-2995
Fax: (302) 998-5785
Website: www.windcrestanimal.com
Hours: 24 hours a day;
        7 days a week;
        365 days a year

Veterinary Emergency Center of
    Delaware (located at Veterinary
    Specialty Center of Delaware)
1212 East Newport Pike
Wilmington, DE 19804
Phone: (302) 691-3647
Fax: (302) 691-3652
Website: www.vscdel.com
Hours: 24 hours a day,
        7 days a week
Note: Please call before arriving.

DISTRICT OF COLUMBIA

Friendship Hospital for Animals
4105 Brandywine Street NW
Washington, DC 20016
Phone: (202) 363-7300
Fax: (202) 363-7126
Website: www.friendshiphospital.com
Hours: 24 hours a day;
7 days a week;
365 days a year

Slinky

"Twice! We never would have guessed that our dear little Lucy, a spunky Blue Heeler, would end up in the E.R. twice. But back in 1999 when we were passing through San Antonio, Texas, was the first time ... for a snake bite (we never expected a rattlesnake right in the city limits). The second time, a year later, was after she chased a squirrel into the street and got hit by a pickup truck. Both incidents were so scary and so traumatic for all of us.

"After the snake bite we rushed Lucy to the nearest clinic we could find but it was closed for the day. Thankfully, an employee cleaning up inside, heard our knock and directed us to an after-hours E.R. We owe so much to the wonderful teams at the pet emergency rooms. It's been seven years since the second visit and Lucy is still with us and we are so happy and thankful for the incredible job the E.R. folks all did for our old girl." ~ John R., Davis, CA

FLORIDA

Boca Raton - *Palm Beach County*
Boca Veterinary Emergency Referral &
    Critical Care Center (located at
    Calusa Veterinary Center)
6900 Congress Avenue
Boca Raton, FL 33487
Phone 1: (561) 999-3000
Phone 2: (561) 443-3699
Fax: (561) 999-3030
Website: www.cvcboca.com
Hours: 24 hours a day; 7 days a week
Note: Daytime practice also at
         this location.

Bradenton - *Manatee County*
Bayshore Animal Hospital
1511 Florida Boulevard
Bradenton, FL 34207
Phone: (941) 756-5544
Fax: --
Website:
    www.bayshoreanimalhospital.biz
Hours: 24 hours
Note: Call before arriving.

Cody

Chelsea

Brandon - *Hillsborough County*
Animal Emergency Clinic of Brandon
Lumsden Executive Park
693 West Lumsden Road
Brandon, FL 33511
Phone: (813) 684-3013
Fax: --
Website: www.myanimaler.com
Hours: Mon - Fri (6pm-8am);
        Weekends from Sat (noon) -
        Mon (8am); Holidays

Brandon Veterinary Specialists
723 West Lumsden Road
Brandon, FL 33511
Phone: (813) 571-3303
Fax: (813) 571-3373
Website:
    www.floridaveterinaryspecialists.com
Hours: 24 hours a day;
        7 days a week;
        365 days a year
Note: Daytime practice also at
         this location.

Casselberry - *Seminole County*
Veterinary Emergency Clinic of
    Central Florida
195 Concord Drive
Casselberry, FL 32707
Phone: (407) 644-4449
Fax: --
Website: www.veconline.com
Hours: Mon - Fri (6pm-7:30am);
        Weekends from Sat (noon) -
        Mon (7:30am); Holidays

Clearwater - *Pinellas County*
Tampa Bay Veterinary Emergency
    Service (located at Tampa Bay
    Veterinary Specialists)
1501 South Belcher Road - Suite 1a
Clearwater, FL 33764
Phone: (727) 535-3500 Main Number
Phone: (727) 531-5752 Emergency
Fax: (727) 539-7865
Website: www.tbvs-inc.com
Hours: Mon - Fri (6pm-8am);
        Weekends from Sat (8am) -
        Mon (8am); Holidays
Note: Daytime practice also at
        this location.

Petey (aka "Sweet-Pea")

Cooper City - *Broward County*
Animal Medical Center (AMC) at
    Cooper City; 24 Hour Emergency -
    Animal Emergency & Critical Care
    Services (AECCS)
9410 Stirling Road
Cooper City, FL 33024
Phone 1: (954) 450-7732 AECCS
Phone 2: (954) 432-5611 AMC
Phone 3: (954) 437-9630
Fax: (954) 437-7207
Website: www.amccc.com
Hours: 24 hours a day;
        7 days a week;
        365 days a year

Coral Springs - *Broward County*
Coral Springs Animal Hospital
    General, Specialty, Emergency &
    Critical Care Hospital
1730 University Drive
Coral Springs, FL 33071
Phone: (954) 753-1800
Fax: --
Website:
    www.coralspringsanimalhosp.com
Hours: 24 hours a day;
        7 days a week;
        365 days a year
Note: Daytime practice also at
        this location.

Daytona Beach - *Volusia County*
Volusia Animal Emergency Clinic
Highway 92
Daytona Beach, FL 32114
Phone: (386) 252-4300
Fax: --
Website: --
Hours: Mon - Thurs (6pm-8am);
        Weekends from Fri (6pm) -
        Mon (8am); Holidays

Deerfield Beach - *Broward County*
Animal Emergency Clinic -
    Deerfield Location
103 North Powerline Road
Deerfield Beach, FL 33442
Phone: (954) 428-9888
Fax: (954) 428-3355
Website: --
Hours: Mon - Thurs (5pm-8am);
        Weekends from Fri (5pm) -
        Mon (8am); Holidays

(Florida continues)

FLORIDA (continued)

Estero - *Lee County*
Florida Veterinary Referral Center &
  24 Hour Emergency and
  Critical Care
9220 Estero Park Commons
Boulevard - Suite 7
Estero, FL 33928
Phone: (239) 992-8878
Fax: (239) 992-0884
Website: www.flvrc.com
Hours: 24 hours a day; 7 days a week

Fort Myers - *Lee County*
Animal ER of SouthWest Florida
15201 North Cleveland Avenue
North Fort Myers, FL 33903
Phone: (239) 995-7755
Fax: --
Website: --
Hours: Mon - Thurs (5pm-8am);
      Weekends from Fri (5pm) to
      Mon (8am); Holidays

Emergency Veterinary Clinic
2045 Collier Avenue
Fort Myers, FL 33901
Phone: (239) 939-5542
Fax: (239) 939-1942
Website: --
Hours: Mon - Thurs (6pm-8am);
      Weekends from Fri (6pm) -
      Mon (8am)

Fort Pierce - *St. Lucie County*
Animal Emergency & Referral Center
3984 South US Route 1
Fort Pierce, FL 34982
Phone: (772) 466-3441
Fax: (772) 466-0206
Website: www.animalemergency.net
Hours: 24 hours a day;
      7 days a week;
      365 days a year

GAINESVILLE - *Alachua County*
University of Florida
Small Animal Hospital
2015 SW 16th Avenue
Gainesville, FL 32610
Phone: (352) 392-2235 Small Animal
Phone: (352) 392-2229 Large Animal
Fax: --
Website: www.vetmed.ufl.edu
Note: As of this writing, it appears
      that emergency services are
      available to current patients
      or referrals.

Gainesville - *Alachua County*
Affiliated Pet Emergency Services, Inc.
7520 West University Avenue
Gainesville, FL 32607
Phone: (352) 373-4444
Fax: --
Website: www.affiliated-pet.com
Hours: Mon - Fri (6pm-8am);
      Weekends from Sat (noon) -
      Mon (8am); Holidays

Holly Hill - *Volusia County*
Animal Emergency Hospital
918 Ridgewood Avenue
Holly Hill, FL 32117
Phone: (386) 252-0206
Fax: (386) 252-0230
Website:
    www.animalemergencyvolusia.com
Hours: Weeknights (5pm-7:30am);
      Weekends & Holidays - 24 hrs

Hollywood - *Broward County*
Hollywood Animal Hospital
2864 Hollywood Boulevard
Hollywood, FL 33020
Phone: (954) 920-3556
Fax: --
Website: www.hollywoodanimal.com
Hours: 24 hours a day;
      7 days a week;
      365 days a year

Kendall - *Miami-Dade County*
Knowles Animal Clinic
9922 Sunset Drive (also known as
South West 72nd Street)
Kendall, FL 33173
Phone: (305) 279-2323
Fax: (305) 279-4002
Website:
    www.knowlesanimalclinics.com
Hours: 24 hours a day;
      7 days a week;
      365 days a year

Jacksonville - *Duval/St. Johns County*
Central Veterinary Emergency
1546 San Marco Boulevard
Jacksonville, FL 32207
Phone: (904) 399-8800
Fax: --
Website: --
Hours: Mon - Fri (6pm-8am);
      Weekends from Sat (noon) -
      Mon (8am)

Jacksonville Animal ER
3444 Southside Boulevard - Suite 101
Jacksonville, FL 32216
Phone: (904) 642-4357
Fax: (904) 642-0868
Website: www.animalerjax.com
Hours: Mon - Thurs (5pm-8am);
      Weekends from Fri (5pm) -
      Mon (8am); Holidays

Jacksonville Beach - *Duval County*
Emergency Pet Clinic
14185 Beach Boulevard
Jacksonville Beach, FL 32250
Phone: (904) 223-8000
Fax: --
Website: --
Hours: Mon - Fri (6pm-8am);
      Weekends from Sat (noon) -
      Mon (8am)

Ginger

Jupiter - *Palm Beach County*
Emergency Pet Care of Jupiter
300 South Central Boulevard
Jupiter, FL 33458
Phone: (561) 746-0555
Fax: --
Website: www.emergencypet.net
Hours: Mon - Thurs (6pm-8am);
      Weekends from Fri (6pm) -
      Mon (8am); Holidays

Lakeland - *Polk County*
Veterinary Emergency Care, Inc.
3609 US Highway 98 South (also
    known as Bartow Highway)
Lakeland, FL 33805
Phone: (863) 665-3199
Fax: (863) 698-2728
Website: --
Hours: Mon - Fri (5:30pm-8am);
      Weekends from Sat (noon) -
      Mon (8am); Holidays

(Florida continues)

FLORIDA (continued)

Largo - *Pinellas County*
Tampa Bay Veterinary Emergency
   Service - Pinellas County Location
1501 South Belcher Road - Suite 1A
Largo, FL 33771
Phone: (727) 535-3500 Main
Phone: (727) 531-5752 Emergency
Fax: (727) 539-7865
Website: www.tampabayves.com
Hours: 24 hours a day; 7 days a week;
    365 days a year

Leesburg - *Lake County*
Veterinary Emergency Clinic of
   Central Florida
33040 Professional Drive
Leesburg, FL 34788
Phone: (352) 728-4440
Fax: --
Website: www.veconline.com
Hours: Mon - Thurs (6pm-7:30am);
    Weekends from Fri (6pm) -
    Mon (7:30am); Holidays

Melbourne - *Brevard County*
Animal Emergency and Critical Care
   Center of Brevard
2281 West Eau Gallie Boulevard
Melbourne, FL 32935
Phone: (321) 725-5365
Fax: --
Website:
   www.centralfloridaanimaler.com
Hours: 24 hours a day; 7 days a week;
    365 days a year

Miami - *Miami-Dade County*
AEC Animal Emergency Clinic South
8429 South West 132nd Street
Miami, FL 33156
Phone: (305) 251-2096
Fax: (305) 254-3207
Website:
   www.aecanimalemergencyclinic.com
Hours: Mon - Fri (6pm-8am);
    Weekends from Sat (noon) -
    Mon (8am); Holidays
Note: Facility will take emergencies
    outside these hours if
    called first.

Knowles Animal Clinic
1000 North West 27th Avenue
Miami, FL 33125
Phone: (305) 649-1234
Fax: (305) 649-1243
Website:
   www.knowlesanimalclinics.com
Hours: 24 hours a day; 7 days a week;
    365 days a year

Miami Veterinary Specialists
8601 Sunset Drive
Miami, FL 33143
Phone: (305) 665-2820
Fax: (305) 665-2821
Website: www.mvshospital.com
Hours: 24 hours a day

Naples - *Collier County*
Emergency Pet Hospital of
   Collier County
6530 Dudley Drive
Naples, FL 34104
Phone: (239) 263-8010
Fax: (239) 263-8455
Website: www.naplesemergencypet.com
Hours: 24 hours a day; 7 days a week

Niceville - *Okaloosa County*
Emergency Veterinary Clinic
212 Government Avenue
Niceville, FL 32578
Phone: (850) 729-3335
Fax: --
Website: --
Hours: Mon - Thurs (6pm-8am);
      Weekends from Fri (6pm) -
      Mon (8am); Holidays

Ocala - *Marion County*
Ocala Animal Emergency Hospital
2182 North East 2nd Street
Ocala, FL 34470
Phone: (352) 840-0044
Fax: --
Website:
   www.ocalaanimalemergency.com
Hours: Mon - Fri (6pm-7am);
      Weekends from Sat (noon) -
      Mon (7am); Holidays

Orange Park - *Clay County*
Clay-Duval Pet Emergency Clinic
275 Corporate Way - Suite 200
Orange Park, FL 32073
Phone: (904) 264-8281
Fax: (904) 264-8997
Website: --
Hours: Mon - Fri (6pm-8am);
      Weekends from Sat (noon) -
      Mon (8am); Holidays

Murphy

Orlando - *Orange County*
Animal Emergency Center
4900 Lake Underhill Road
   (temporary address)
Orlando, FL 32822
Phone: (407) 273-3336
Fax: (407) 273-3338
Website: www.pet-er.org
Hours: Mon - Fri (6pm-7:30am);
      Weekends from Sat (noon) -
      Mon (7:30am); Holidays

Veterinary Emergency Clinic of
   Central Florida
2080 Principal Row
Orlando, FL 32837
Phone: (407) 438-4449
Fax: (407) 857-3666
Website: www.veconline.com
Hours: Mon - Fri (6pm-7:30am);
      Weekends from Sat (noon) -
      Mon (7:30am); Holidays

Oviedo - *Seminole County*
Aloma Jancy Animal Hospital
3370 Pet Country Court
Oviedo, FL 32765
Phone: (407) 671-1183
Fax: (407) 671-8219
Website:
   www.alomajancyanimalhospital.com
Hours: 24 hours a day staffed; Call.

Palm Beach Gardens -
   Palm Beach County
Pet Emergency of Palm Beach County
3816 Northlake Boulevard
Palm Beach Gardens, FL 33403
Phone: (561) 691-9999
Fax: --
Website: --
Hours: 24 hours a day; 7 days a week

(Florida continues)

FLORIDA (continued)

Palm Harbor - *Pinellas County*
A.A.Animal ER Center, LLC
36401 US Highway 19 North
Palm Harbor, Florida 34684
Phone: (727) 787-5402
Fax: --
Website: --
Hours: Weeknights (5:30pm-8am);
Weekends & Major Holidays -
24 hours

Animal Emergency of Countryside
30606 US Highway 19 North
Palm Harbor, FL 34684
Phone: (727) 786-5755
Fax: --
Website: www.emergencyanimal.com
Hours: Mon - Fri (5:30pm-7am);
Sat & Sun & Holidays - 24 hrs

Pembroke Pines - *Broward County*
St. Francis Emergency Animal Hospital
6602 Pines Boulevard
Pembroke Pines, FL 33024
Phone: (954) 962-0300
Fax: --
Website:
www.stfrancisemergency.com
Hours: 24 hours a day;
7 days a week;
365 days a year

Pensacola - *Escambia County*
Veterinary Emergency Referral Center
3998 North Palafox Street
Pensacola, FL 32505
Phone: (850) 434-2924
Fax: --
Website: --
Hours: Mon - Thurs (6pm-8am);
Weekends from Fri (6pm) -
Mon (8am); Holidays

Port Charlotte - *Charlotte County*
Veterinary Emergency Clinic
17829 Murdock Circle
Port Charlotte, FL 33948
Phone: (941) 255-5222
Fax: --
Website: --
Hours: Mon - Fri (5pm-8am);
Sat & Sun & Holidays - 24 hrs

Port Richey - *Pasco County*
Animal Emergency Of Pasco
8740 US Highway 19
Port Richey, FL 34668
Phone: (727) 841-6575
Fax: --
Website: --
Hours: Mon - Thurs (5:30pm-8am);
Weekends from Fri (5:30pm)
to Mon (8am); Holidays

Rockledge - *Brevard County*
Animal Specialty Hospital and
Emergency Clinic
5775 Schenck Avenue
Rockledge, FL 32955
Phone: (321) 752-7600
Fax: --
Website: --
Hours: Weeknights (6pm-8am);
Weekends & Holidays - 24 hrs

St. Augustine - *St. Johns County*
Animal Emergency Hospital
2505 Old Moultrie Road
Saint Augustine, FL 32086
Phone: (904) 794-5071
Fax: --
Website:
www.animalemergencyofstjohns.com
Hours: Mon - Thurs (5pm-7:30am);
Weekends & Holidays - 24 hrs

St. Petersburg - *Pinellas County*
Animal Emergency Clinic of
    St. Petersburg
3165 22nd Avenue North
St. Petersburg, FL 33713
Phone: (727) 323-1311
Fax: --
Web: --
Hours: 24 hours a day; 7 days a week

Noah's Place 24-Hour Animal
    Medical Center
2050 62nd Avenue North
St. Petersburg, FL 33702
Phone: (727) 522-6640
Fax: (727) 525-6327
Website: www.noahs24.com
Hours: 24 hours a day

Keets

Sarasota - *Sarasota County*
Emergency Veterinary Clinic
7517 South Tamiami Trail
Sarasota, FL 34231
Phone: (941) 923-7260
Fax: --
Website: --
Hours: Mon - Fri (5pm-8am);
        Sat & Sun & Holidays - 24 hrs

Spring Hill - *Hernando County*
Animal Emergency Of Hernando
3496 Deltona Boulevard
Spring Hill, FL 34606
Phone: (352) 666-0904
Fax: --
Website: --
Hours: Mon - Fri (5:30pm-8am);
        Weekends from Sat (8pm) -
        Mon (8am); Holidays

Stuart - *Martin County*
Pet Emergency & Critical Care Clinic
2239 South Kanner Highway
Stuart, FL 34994
Phone: (772) 781-3302
Fax: --
Website: --
Hours: Mon - Fri (6pm-7am);
        Sat & Sun & Holidays - 24 hrs

Tallahassee - *Leon County*
All Pets Emergency Treatment (located
    at Northwood Animal Hospital)
1881 North Martin Luther King Jr Blvd.
Tallahassee, FL 32303
Phone: (850) 385-7387 Emergency
Phone: (850) 385-8181 Main Phone
Fax: --
Website: --
Hours: 24 hours a day; 7 days a week
Note: Daytime practice also at
        this location.

(Florida continues)

FLORIDA (continued)

Tampa - *Hillsborough County*
Florida Veterinary Specialists
3000 Busch Lake Boulevard
Tampa, FL 33614
Phone: (813) 933-8944
Fax: (813) 936-9595
Website:
  www.floridaveterinaryspecialists.com
Hours: 24 hours a day; 7 days a week;
       365 days a year

Tampa Bay Veterinary Emergency
  Service - Hillsborough County
  Location
238 East Bearss Avenue
Tampa, FL 33613
Phone: (813) 265-4043
Fax: (813) 962-4477
Website: www.tampabayves.com
Hours: Mon - Fri (6pm-8am);
       Weekends from Sat (noon) -
       Mon (8am); Holidays

Westchase Veterinary Center &
  Emergency Clinic
11659 Country Way Boulevard
Tampa, FL 33635
Phone: (813) 818-0087
Fax: --
Website: --
Hours: Call for updated emergency
       hours.
Note: Daytime practice also at
      this location.

Magic

University Park - *Manatee County*
Animal ER of University Park
  Sarasota/Bradenton
8237 Cooper Creek Boulevard
University Park, FL 34201
Phone: (941) 355-2884
Fax: (941) 359-9470
Website:
  www.universityanimalclinic.net
Hours: Mon - Fri (6pm 7:30am);
       Sat & Sun & Holidays - 24 hrs
Note: Opens when adjacent
      clinic closes.

West Palm - *Palm Beach County*
Palm Beach Veterinary Referral and
  Critical Care
3092 Forest Hills Boulevard
West Palm Beach, FL 33064
Phone: (561) 434-5700
Fax: --
Website: --
Hours: 24 hours a day; 7 days a week

Pet Emergency of Palm Beach County
3816 Northlake Boulevard
West Palm Beach, FL 33403
Phone: (561) 691-9999
Fax: --
Website: --
Hours: Call for updated
       emergency hours.

Winter Park - *Orange County*
Veterinary Emergency Care, Inc.
100 Orange Blossom Court
Winter Park, FL 32792
Phone: (863) 698-2728
Fax: --
Website: --
Hours: Mon - Fri (5:30pm-8am);
       Weekends from Sat (noon) -
       Mon (8am); Holidays

GEORGIA

Alpharetta - *Fulton County*
All Pets Emergency and
    Referral Center P.C.
6460 Highway 9 North
Alpharetta, GA 30004
Phone: (678) 366-2500
Fax: --
Website: www.aperc.com
Hours: 24 hours a day;
    7 days a week

ATHENS - *Clarke County*
University of Georgia
College of Veterinary Medicine
Carlton Street
Athens, GA 30602
Phone: (706) 542-3221
Website: www.vet.uga.edu
Note: Call to discuss any
    emergency.

Atlanta - *Fulton County*
Georgia Veterinary Specialists and
    Emergency Care
455 Abernathy Road NE
Atlanta, GA 30328
Phone: (404) 459-0903
Fax: (404) 459-6462
Website: www.gvsvet.com
Hours: 24 hours a day;
    7 days a week

Pets are People, too VH Ansley
1510 Piedmont Avenue
Atlanta, GA 30324
Phone: (404) 875-7387
Fax: --
Website: www.petsarepeopletoo.net
Hours: Staffed 24 hours;
    emergencies accepted
    midnight to 7:30am.
    Call.

Augusta - *Augusta-Richmond County*
Augusta Animal Emergency Clinic
208 Hudson Trace
Augusta, GA 30907
Phone: (706) 733-7458
Toll Free: (800) 527-0149
Fax: --
Website: --
Hours: After Hours, Weekends,
    Holidays

St. Francis Animal Hospital
2647 Perimeter Parkway
Augusta, GA 30909
Phone: (706) 860-6617
Fax: --
Website: www.sfah.net
Hours: 24 hours a day; 7 days a week
Note: Daytime practice also at
    this location.

Chamblee - *DeKalb County*
Pets are People, too VH Dunwoody
4280 North Peachtree Road
Chamblee, GA 30341
Phone: (770) 452-1001
Fax: --
Website: www.petsarepeopletoo.net
Hours: Staffed 24 hours;
    emergencies accepted
    midnight to 7:30am. Call.

(Georgia continues)

Pumpkin

GEORGIA (continued)

Columbus - *Muscogee County*
Animal Emergency Center
2509 Manchester Expressway
Columbus, GA 31904
Phone: (706) 324-6659
Fax: (706) 324-2727
Website: --
Hours: Mon - Fri (6pm-8am);
  Weekends from Sat (noon) -
  Mon (8am)

Fayetteville - *Fayette County*
Southern Crescent Animal
 Emergency Clinic
1270 Highway 54 East
Fayetteville, GA 30214
Phone: (770) 460-8166
Fax: --
Website: --
Hours: Mon - Thurs (6pm-8am);
  Weekends from Fri (6pm) -
  Mon (8am); Holidays

Sugar

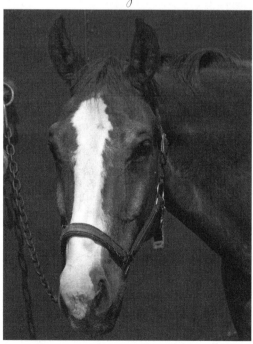

Gainesville - *Hall County*
An-Emerge Animal Emergency Clinic
275 Pearl Nix Parkway
Gainesville, Georgia 30501
Phone: (770) 534-2911
Fax: (770) 287-8993
Website: --
Hours: Mon - Fri (6pm-8am);
  Weekends from Sat (noon) -
  Mon (8am); Holidays

Lawrenceville - *Gwinnett County*
Animal Emergency Center
 of Gwinnett
1956 Lawrenceville-Suwanee Road
Lawrenceville, GA 30043
Phone: (770) 277-3220
Fax: --
Website: www.aecog.com
Hours: Mon - Fri (6pm-8am);
  Weekends from Sat (noon) -
  Mon (8am); Holidays

Lilburn - *Gwinnett County*
Pets are People, too VH Gwinnett
470 Pleasant Hill Road
Lilburn, GA 30047
Phone: (770) 923-7474
Fax: --
Website: www.petsarepeopletoo.net
Hours: Emergencies 7 days a week

Lithia Springs - *Douglas County*
Westside Animal Emergency Clinic
591 Thornton Road
Lithia Springs, GA 30116
Phone: (770) 819-1090
Fax: --
Website: --
Hours: Mon - Fri (6pm-8am);
  Weekends from Sat (noon) -
  Mon (8am)

Loganville - *Walton County*
Eastside Animal Emergency Center
2715 Loganville Highway 20
Loganville, GA 30052
Phone: (678) 985-5530
Fax: --
Website: --
Hours: 24 hours a day; 7 days a week

Macon - *Bibb County*
Animal Emergency Care
2009 Mercer University Drive
Macon, GA 31204
Phone: (478) 750-0911
Fax: --
Website: --
Hours: Mon - Fri (6pm-9am);
Sat (1pm) - Sun (10am);
Sun (1pm) - Mon morning

Sparky

Marietta - *Cobb County*
Cobb Emergency Veterinary Clinic
630 Cobb Parkway North
Marietta, GA 30062
Phone: (770) 424-9157
Fax: (770) 424-8064
Website: www.cobbevc.com
Hours: 24 hours a day; 7 days a week

Roswell - *Fulton County*
Animal Emergency Center of
North Fulton
900 Mansell Road
Roswell, GA 30076
Phone: (770) 594-2266
Fax: --
Website: --
Hours: Mon - Fri (6pm-8am);
Weekends from Sat (noon) -
Mon (8am); Holidays

Pets are People, too VH Roswell
535 Sun Valley Drive
Roswell, GA 30076
Phone: (770) 993-3040
Fax: --
Website: www.petsarepeopletoo.net
Hours: Emergencies 7 days a week

Sandy Springs - *Fulton County*
Animal Emergency Center of
Sandy Springs
228 Sandy Springs Place
Sandy Springs, GA 30328
Phone: (404) 252-7881
Fax: --
Website: --
Hours: Mon - Thurs (6pm-8am);
Weekends from Fri (6pm) -
Mon (8am); Holidays

Savannah - *Chatham County*
Savannah Veterinary Emergency Clinic
317 Eisenhower Drive
Savannah, GA 31406
Phone: (912) 355-6113
Fax: (912) 355-4221
Website: --
Hours: Mon - Fri (6pm-8am); Sat &
Sun & Holidays - 24 hours

(Georgia continues)

GEORGIA (continued)

Tucker - *DeKalb County*
Dekalb-Gwinnett Animal
   Emergency Clinic
6430 Lawrenceville Highway
Tucker, GA 30084
Phone: (770) 491-0661
Fax: (770) 978-0542
Website: www.dgaec.com
Hours: Mon - Thurs (6pm-9am);
      Weekends & Holidays - 24 hrs

Pets are People, too VH Northlake
2015 Montreal Road
Tucker, GA 30084
Phone: (770) 493-1001
Fax: --
Website: www.petsarepeopletoo.net
Hours: Emergencies 7 days a week

Union City - *Fulton County*
Union City Medical Center and
   Emergency Clinic
6702 Shannon Parkway
Union City, GA 30291
Phone: (770) 964-0700
Fax: --
Website: --
Hours: 24 hours a day

Watkinsville - *Oconee County*
Animal Emergency Hospital
7530 Macon Highway
Watkinsville, GA 30677
Phone: (706) 769-0229
Fax: --
Website: --
Hours: Mon - Thurs (6pm-8am);
      Weekends from Fri (6pm) -
      Mon (8am)

Woodstock - *Cherokee County*
Cherokee Emergency Veterinary Clinic
7800 Highway 92
Woodstock, GA 30189
Phone: (770) 924-3720
Fax: (770) 924-3721
Website: www.cobbevc.com
Hours: Mon - Thurs (6pm-8am);
      Weekends from Fri (6pm) -
      Mon (8am)

Bonnie and Slipper

HAWAII

Please Note: The State of Hawaii has a state quarantine on pets. If traveling to Hawaii, please become familiar with their state quarantine requirements before arriving.

Aiea - *Honolulu County*
Animal Clinic Waipahu
98-020 Kamehameha Highway
Aiea, HI 96701
Phone: (808) 487-3607
Fax: --
Website: --
Hours: 24 hour emergency

Waipahu - *Honolulu County*
Animal Clinic Waipahu
94-806 Moloalo Street
Waipahu, HI 96797
Phone: (808) 671-1751
Fax: --
Website: --
Hours: Doctors & Staff at hospital
        24 hours a day

Rocky (on the road to recovery!)

IDAHO

Boise - **Garden City** - *Ada County*
WESTVET Animal Emergency &
   Specialty Center
5019 North Sawyer Avenue
Garden City, ID 83714
Phone: (208) 375-1600
Fax: (208) 375-1606
Website: www.westvet.net
Hours: 24 hours a day;
      7 days a week;
      365 days a year

Meridian - *Ada County*
All Valley Animal Care Center/
   Emergency Care
2326 East Cinema Drive
Meridian, ID 83642
Phone: (208) 888-0818
Fax: --
Website: www.allvalleypet.com
Hours: 24 hours a day;
      7 days a week

WESTVET Meridian
   Animal Emergency
3085 East Magic View Drive -
   Suite 110
Meridian, ID 83642
Phone: (208) 288-0400
Fax: --
Website: www.westvet.net
Hours: Mon - Fri (5:30pm-8:30am);
      Sat & Sun & Holidays - 24 hrs

Post Falls - *Kootenai County*
North Idaho Pet Emergency
2700 East Seltice Way
Post Falls, ID 83854
Phone: (208) 777-2707
Fax: --
Website: --
Hours: 24 hours a day; 7 days a week

Beau

ILLINOIS

Aurora - *Kane County*
VCA Aurora Animal Hospital
2600 West Galena Boulevard
Aurora, IL 60506
Phone: (630) 896-8541
Fax: (630) 896-8594
Website: www.vcaaurora.com
Hours: Mon - Fri (6pm-8am);
　　　Weekends from Sat (4pm) -
　　　Mon (8am)

Berwyn - *Cook County*
Berwyn Animal Hospital - VCA
2845 South Harlem Avenue
Berwyn, IL 60402
Phone: (708) 749-4200
Fax: (708) 749-1716
Website: www.vcaberwyn.com
Hours: Mon - Fri (8pm-8am);
　　　Weekends from Sat (4pm) -
　　　Mon (8am)

Bloomington - *McClean County*
Animal Emergency Clinic (AEC)
2505 East Oakland Avenue
Bloomington, Illinois 61701
Phone: (309) 665-5020
Fax: (309) 665-5021
Website: --
Hours: Mon - Fri (6pm-8am);
　　　Weekends from Sat (noon) -
　　　Mon (8am); Holidays

Buffalo Grove - *Lake County*
Veterinary Specialty Center
1515 Busch Parkway
Buffalo Grove, IL 60089
Phone: (847) 459-7535
Main Fax: (847) 808-8900
Fax: --
Website: www.vetspecialty.com
Hours: 24 hours a day; 7 days a week;
　　　365 days a year

Champaign - *Champaign County*
Animal Emergency Clinic of
　　Champaign County
1713 South State Street
Champaign, IL 61820
Phone: (217) 359-1977
Fax: --
Website: --
Hours: Weekdays (6pm-8am);
　　　Weekends & Holidays - 24 hrs

Radar Love (getting his shots)

Chicago - *Cook County*
Chicago Veterinary Emergency Services
3123 North Clybourn Avenue
Chicago, IL 60618
Phone: (773) 281-7110
Fax: --
Website:
www.chicagoveterinaryemergency.com
Hours: Mon - Fri (7pm-8am);
　　　Weekends from Sat (noon) -
　　　Mon (8am)

Chicago Pet Transportation:

Chicago Pet Chauffeurs
Phone: (773) 665-2327
Emergency Service Available
Website:
　　www.chicagopetchauffeurs.com

Paws Around Chicago
Phone: (773) 278-1937
Emergency Pet Transport

(Illinois continues)

ILLINOIS (continued)

Collinsville - *Madison County*
Animal Emergency Center
2005 Mall Street
Collinsville, IL 62234
Phone: (618) 346-1843
Fax: --
Website: --
Hours: Mon - Fri (6pm-8am);
Weekends from Sat (noon) -
Mon (8am); Holidays

Crestwood - *Cook County*
Emergency Veterinary Care South
13715 South Cicero Avenue
Crestwood, IL 60445
Phone: (708) 388-3771
Fax: (708) 388-3795
Website: www.evcs.vetsuite.com
Hours: Mon - Fri (7pm-8am);
Weekends from Sat (1pm) -
Mon (8am); Holidays

Crystal Lake - *McHenry County*
Animal Emergency Clinic
280 Virginia Road
Crystal Lake, IL 60014
Phone: (815) 479-9119
Fax: (815) 479-0919
Website:
www.myvetonline.com/website/aemc/
Hours: Mon - Thurs (6pm-8am);
Weekends from Fri (6pm) -
Mon (8am)

Downers Grove - *DuPage County*
Arboretum View Animal Hospital
2551 Warrenville Road
Downers Grove, IL 60515
Phone: (630) 963-0424
Fax: (630) 963-0537
Website:
www.arboretumviewanimalhospital.com
Hours: 24 hours a day

Dundee - *Kane County*
Dundee Animal Hospital
199 Penny Avenue
Dundee, IL 60118
Phone: (847) 428-6114
Fax: (847) 428-0177
Website:
www.dundeeanimalhospital.com
Hours: 24 hours a day; 7 days a week

Elmwood Park - *Cook County*
Midwest Animal Emergency Hospital
(located at Midwest Bird and Exotic
Animal Hospital)
7510 West North Avenue
Elmwood Park, IL 60707
Phone: (708) 453-4755
Phone: (708) 453-8181 Midwest Exotic
Fax: (708) 453-8194
Website:
www.midwestexotichospital.com
Hours: Mon - Fri (7pm-8am);
Weekends from Sat (2pm) -
Mon (8am); Holidays
Note: Emergency Services for cats,
dogs, and exotics.

Grayslake - *Lake County*
All Creatures Emergency
1806 East Belvidere Road
Grayslake, IL 60030
Phone: (847) 548-5300
Fax: (847) 548-5347
Website: --
Hours: 24 hours a day

Jake (der Wiggler)

Lisle - *DuPage County*
Emergency Veterinary Service
820 Ogden Avenue
Lisle, IL 60532
Phone: (630) 960-2900
Fax: --
Website: --
Hours: Mon - Fri (6pm-8am);
     Weekends from Sat (noon) -
     Mon (8am)

Mokena - *Will County*
Animal Emergency of Mokena
19110 88th Avenue
Mokena, IL 60448
Phone: (708) 326-4800
Fax: (708) 326-3906
Web:
 www.animalemergencyofmokena.com
Hours: Mon - Fri (7pm-8am);
     Weekends from Sat (1pm) -
     Mon (8am); Holidays

Northbrook - *Cook County*
Animal Emergency and
   Referral Center (AERC)
1810 Skokie Boulevard
Northbrook, IL 60062
Phone: (847) 564-5775
Fax: (847) 564-5899
Website: www.aeccc.com
Hours: 24 hours a day;
     7 days a week;
     365 days a year

Rockford - *Winnebago County*
Animal Emergency Clinic of Rockford
4236 Maray Drive
Rockford, IL 61107
Phone: (815) 229-7791
Fax: --
Website: --
Hours: 24 hours a day; 7 days a week

Raider

Schaumburg - *Cook County*
Golf Rose Animal Hospital &
   Animal Emergency Service
1375 North Roselle Road
Schaumburg, IL 60195
Phone: (847) 885-4050
   Emergency Service
Phone: (847) 885-3344
   Animal Hospital
Fax: (847) 885-8352
Web: www.golfroseah.com
Hours: 24 hours a day; 7 days a week

Skokie - *Cook County*
Animal 911
3735 Dempster Street
Skokie, IL 60076
Phone: (847) 673-9110
Fax: --
Website: --
Hours: Mon - Fri (5pm-8am);
     Weekends from Sat (noon) -
     Mon (8am)

(Illinois continues)

ILLINOIS (continued)

St. Charles - *Kane County*
Emergency Veterinary Services of
  St. Charles
530 Dunham Road
St. Charles, IL 60174
Phone: (630) 584-7447
Fax 1: (630) 584-2697
Fax 2: (630) 584-3545
Website:
  www.emergencyvetservices.com
Hours: Mon - Fri (6pm-8am);
    Weekends from Sat (noon) -
    Mon (8am); Holidays

URBANA - *Champaign County*
University of Illinois
Veterinary Teaching Hospital
  Small Animal Clinic
1008 West Hazelwood Drive
Urbana, IL 61802
Phone: (217) 333-5300
  Small Animal Emergency
Phone: (217) 333-2000
  Large Animal Emergency
Website: www.cvm.uiuc.edu
Note: Call to discuss any emergency.

Winston on a bad day

INDIANA

Anderson - *Madison County*
VCA Northwood Animal Hospital
3255 North State Road 9
Anderson, IN 46012
Phone: (765) 649-5218
Fax: (765) 649-5220
Website: www.vcanorthwood.com
Hours: 24 hours a day

Evansville - *Vanderburgh County*
All Pet Emergency Clinic
104 South Heidelbach Avenue
Evansville, IN 47713
Phone: (812) 422-3300
Fax: --
Website: --
Hours: Mon - Fri (6pm-8am);
       Weekends from Sat (noon) -
       Mon (8am)

Fort Wayne - *Allen County*
Northeast Indiana Veterinary
   Emergency and Specialty Hospital
5818 Maplecrest Road
Fort Wayne, IN 46835
Phone: (260) 426-1062
Fax: (260) 485-0130
Website: --
Hours: 24 hours a day

Indianapolis - *Marion County*
Airport Animal Emergi-Center
5235 West Washington Street
Indianapolis, IN 46241
Phone: (317) 248-0832
Fax: --
Website: --
Hours: Mon - Fri (6pm-8am);
       Weekends from Sat (noon) -
       Mon (8am)

Animal Emergency Center of
   Indianapolis (located at Indiana
   Veterinary Specialists)
8250 Bash Street
Indianapolis, IN 46250
Phone: (317) 849-4925 Emergency
Phone: (317) 841-3606 Main Number
Fax: (317) 576-8052
Website: www.indyvetspecialists.com
Hours: 24 hours a day; 7 days a week
Note: Daytime practice also at
        this location.

Indianapolis Veterinary Emergency
   Center (IVEC)
5425 Victory Drive
Indianapolis , IN 46203
Phone: (317) 782-4418 Emergency
Toll Free: (800) 551-4879
Fax: (317) 786-4484
Website: www.indyvet.com
Hours: 24 hours a day;
       7 days a week;
       365 days year

Noah's Animal Hospital &
   24 Hour Emergency Center
5510 Millersville Road
Indianapolis , IN 46226
Phone 1: (317) 253-1327
Phone 2: (317) 244-7738
Fax: (317) 726-2404
Website: www.noahshospitals.com
Hours: 24 hours a day

VCA West 86th St. Animal Hospital
4030 West 86th Street
Indianapolis, IN 46268
Phone: (317) 872-0200
Fax: (317) 872-0226
Website: www.vcawest86thstreet.com
Hours: 24 hours a day; 7 days a week

(Indiana continues)

INDIANA (continued)

Lafayette - *Tippecanoe County*
Animal Emergency Clinic
1343 Sagamore Parkway North
Lafayette, IN 47904
Phone: (765) 449-2001
Fax: --
Website: --
Hours: Mon - Thurs (6pm-8am);
    Weekends from Fri (6pm) -
    Mon (8am)

Schererville - *Lake County*
Calumet Emergency Vet Clinic
216 West US Highway 30
    (also known as Lincoln Highway)
Schererville, IN 46375
Phone: (219) 865-0970
Fax: (219) 865-0972
Website: --
Hours: Mon - Fri (6pm-8am);
    Weekends from Sat (noon) -
    Mon (8am); Holidays

Princess

South Bend - *St. Joseph County*
Animal Emergency Clinic
17903 State Road 23
South Bend, IN 46635
Phone: (574) 259-8387
Fax: --
Website: --
Hours: Mon - Thurs (6pm-7:30am);
    Weekends from Fri (6pm) -
    Mon (7:30am); Holidays

Terre Haute - *Vigo County*
Animal Emergency Clinic
1238 South 3rd Street
Terre Haute, IN 47802
Phone: (812) 242-2273
Fax: --
Website: --
Hours: New facility 2007; Call for
    updated emergency hours.

WEST LAFAYETTE -
    Tippecanoe County
Purdue University
625 Harrison Street
West Lafayette, IN 47907
Phone: (765) 494-7607
Phone: (765) 494-1107
    Small Animal Hospital
Phone: (765) 494-8548
    Large Animal Hospital
Website: www.vet.purdue.edu
Note: At the time of this writing, a
    referral is needed for the
    Small Animal Hospital.

Westville - *LaPorte County*
North Central Veterinary
    Emergency Center
1645 South US Highway 421
Westville, IN 46391
Phone: (219) 785-7300
Fax: (219) 785-7314
Website: www.ncvec.pnc.edu
Hours: Mon - Fri (5pm-8am);
    Weekends from Sat (8am) -
    Mon (8am); Holidays
Note: Located on Purdue
    University's North Central
    Campus.

IOWA

AMES - *Story County*
Iowa State University
Veterinary Clinical Sciences
Veterinary Teaching Hospital
1600 South 16th Street
Ames, IA 50010
Phone: (515) 294-4900
Fax: (515) 294-7520
Website: www.vetmed.iastate.edu
Hours: Open for emergencies 24 hours
Note: Regular appointments
    also available.

Bettendorf - *Scott County*
Animal Emergency Center of
  the Quad Cities
1510 State Street
Bettendorf, IA 52722
Phone: (563) 344-9599
Fax: (563) 344-0221
Website: www.qcanimaler.org
Hours: Mon - Fri (5pm-8am);
    Weekends from Sat (noon) -
    Mon (8am); Holidays

Newton

Cedar Rapids - *Linn County*
Eastern Iowa Veterinary
  Specialty Center
755 Capital Drive SW
Cedar Rapids, IA 52404
Phone: (319) 841-5161
Fax: --
Website: --
Hours: 24 hours a day; 7 days a week

Des Moines - *Polk County*
The Animal Emergency &
  Referral Center of Central Iowa
6110 Creston Avenue
Des Moines, IA 50321
Phone: (515) 280-3051
Fax: (515) 280-3718
Website: www.aecdsm.com
Hours: Mon - Thurs (5:30pm-7:30am);
    Weekends from Fri (5:30pm) -
    Mon (8:30am); Holidays

Iowa City - *Johnson County*
Emergency Veterinary Service of
  Iowa City (located at Bright Eyes &
  Bushy Tails Veterinary Hospital)
3030 Northgate Avenue
Iowa City, IA 52245
Phone: (319) 351-4256
Fax: --
Website: www.bebt.com
Hours: 24 hours a day; 7 days a week

KANSAS

MANHATTAN - *Riley County*
Kansas State University
College of Veterinary Medicine
101 Trotter Hall
Manhattan, KS 66506
Phone: (785) 532-5690 Small Animal
Phone: (785) 532-5700 Large Animal
Website: www.vet.ksu.edu
Hours: Emergency and Critical Care
available 24 hours a day.

Mission - *Johnson County*
Mission MedVet
5914 Johnson Drive
Mission, KS 66202
Phone: (913) 722-5566
Toll Free: (800) 790-7766
Fax: (913) 722-1890
Website: www.missionmedvet.com
Hours: 24 hours a day;
7 days a week;
365 days a year

Sasha and Missy

Overland Park - *Johnson County*
Veterinary Specialty and
Emergency Center
11950 West 110th Street
Overland Park, KS 66210
Phone: (913) 642-9563
Toll Free: (800) 413-6851
Fax: (913) 381-0421
Website: www.vseckc.com
Hours: 24 hours a day;
7 days a week;
365 days a year

Topeka - *Shawnee County*
Emergency Animal Clinic of Topeka
839 South West Fairlawn Road
Topeka, KS 66606
Phone: (785) 272-2926
Toll Free: (866) 878-2926
Fax: --
Website: --
Hours: Mon - Fri (5:30pm-8am);
Weekends from Sat (noon) -
Mon (8am); Holidays

Wichita - *Sedgwick County*
Veterinary Emergency &
Specialty Hospital of Wichita
727 South Washington Street
Wichita, KS 67211
Phone: (316) 262-5321
Fax: (316) 262-8305
Website: --
Hours: 24 hours a day

KENTUCKY

Lexington - *Fayette County*
AA Small Animal Emergency Service
200 Southland Drive
Lexington, KY 40503
Phone: (859) 276-2505
Fax: (859) 278-2719
Website:
   www.smallanimalemergency.com
Hours: Mon - Fri (6pm-8am);
     Weekends from Sat (8am) -
     Mon (8am)

Louisville - *Jefferson County*
Animal Emergency Center & Hospital
3321 Red Roof Inn Place
Louisville, KY 40218
Phone: (502) 456-6102
Fax: --
Web: www.louisvillepeter.com
Hours: Mon - Sat (6pm-8am);
     Weekends from Sat (8pm) -
     Mon (8am); Holidays

Associated Veterinary Specialists
1000 Lyndon Lane
Louisville, KY 40222
Phone: (502) 423-1700
Fax: --
Website: --
Hours: 24 hours a day; 7 days a week

Jefferson Animal Hospital &
   Emergency Center
   24 Hour Emergency Trauma Center
4504 Outer Loop
Louisville , KY 40219
Phone: (502) 966-4104
Fax: (502) 966-3904
Website:
   www.jeffersonanimalhospital.com
Hours: 24 hours a day; 7 days a week;
     365 days a year

Louisville Veterinary Specialty and
   Emergency Services
12905 Shelbyville Road - Suite 3
Louisville, KY 40243
Phone: (502) 244-3036
Fax: (502) 244-3046
Website: www.lvses.com
Hours: 24 hours a day; 7 days a week;
     365 days a year

Taylor Mill - *Kenton County*
OKI Veterinary Emergency and
   Critical Care
5052 Old Taylor Mill Road
Taylor Mill, KY 41015
Phone: (606) 261-9900
Fax: (606) 261-9900
Website: www.vss.org
Hours: Mon - Fri (6pm-8am);
     Weekends from Sat (noon) -
     Mon (8am)

Wilder - *Campbell County*
Greater Cincinnati Veterinary
   Specialty & Emergency Services
11 Beacon Drive
Wilder, KY 41076
Phone: (859) 572-0560
Fax: (859) 572-0561
Website: www.petveter.com
Hours: Mon - Fri (6pm-8am);
     Weekends from Sat (noon) -
     Mon (8am); Holidays

Scooter

LOUISANA

Alexandria - *Rapides Parish*
Crossroads Animal Emergency Clinic
5405 North Boulevard
Alexandria, LA 71301
Phone: (318) 427-1292
Fax: --
Website: --
Hours: Open weekends. Call.

Nugent

BATON ROUGE -
East Baton Rouge Parish
Louisiana State University
LSU School of Veterinary Medicine
Skip Bertman Drive
Baton Rouge, LA 70803
Phone: (225) 578-9600
   Small Animals Emergency
Phone: (225) 578-9500
   Large Animals Emergency
Fax: (225) 578-9916
Website: www.vetmed.lsu.edu
Hours: Emergencies addressed
     24 hours a day.
Note: Routine appointments
     also available.

Baton Rouge -
East Baton Rouge Parish
Baton Rouge Pet Emergency Hospital
1514 Cottondale Drive
Baton Rouge, LA 70815
Phone: (225) 925-5566
Fax: --
Website: --
Hours: 24 hours a day

Lafayette - *Lafayette Parish*
Lafayette Animal Emergency Clinic
206 Winchester Drive
Lafayette, LA 70506
Phone: (337) 989-0992
Fax: --
Website: --
Hours: Mon - Fri (5pm-8am);
     Weekends from Sat (noon) -
     Mon (8am)

Lake Charles - *Calcasieu Parish*
Pet Emergency Clinic of
   South West Louisana
1501 West McNeese Street
Lake Charles, LA 70605
Phone: (337) 562-0400
Fax: --
Website: --
Hours: Mon - Fri (5:30pm-7am);
     Weekends from Sat (noon) -
     Mon (7am); Holidays

LaPlace - *St. John the Baptist Parish*
Riverlands Animal Hospital
1112 West Airline Highway
LaPlace, LA 70068
Phone: (985) 652-6369
Fax: (985) 653-7522
Website:
   www.riverlandsanimalhospital.com
Hours: 24 hours a day; 7 days a week
Note: Daytime practice also at
     this location.

Mandeville - *St. Tammany Parish*
Louisiana Veterinary Referral Center
2611 Florida Street
Mandeville, LA 70448
Phone: (985) 626-4862
Fax: --
Website: --
Hours: 24 hours a day
Note: Center is a Referral Clinic
from Mon - Fri (7am-6pm).

Metairie - *Jefferson Parish*
Animal Emergency Clinic, Inc.
1955 Veterans Memorial Boulevard
Metairie, LA 70005
Phone: (504) 835-8508
Fax: --
Website: --
Hours: Mon - Fri (6pm-8am);
Weekends from Sat (1pm) -
Mon (8am)

Southeast Veterinary Emergency and
Critical Care
400 North Causeway Boulevard
Metairie, LA 70001
Phone: (504) 219-0444
Fax: --
Website: --
Hours: 24 hours a day

Flo

New Orleans - *Jefferson Parish*
Animal Medical Clinic
4738 Magazine Street
New Orleans, LA 70115
Phone: (504) 891-1411
Fax: --
Website: --
Hours: 24 hours a day

Shreveport - *Caddo Parish*
Animal Emergency Clinic of
Shreveport-Bossier, Inc.
2421 Warren Avenue
Shreveport, LA 71104
Phone: (318) 227-2345
Fax: --
Website:
Hours: Mon - Fri (6pm-8am);
Weekends from Sat (noon) -
Mon (8am)

Terrytown - *Jefferson Parish*
Westbank Pet Emergency Clinic
1152 Terry Parkway
Terrytown, LA 70056
Phone: (504) 392-1932
Fax: --
Website: --
Hours: Mon - Fri (6pm-8am);
Weekends from Sat (noon) -
Mon (8am); Holidays

West Monroe - *Ouachita Parish*
Animal Emergency Clinic of
North East Louisana
102 Downing Pines Road
West Monroe, LA 71292
Phone: (318) 410-0555
Fax: --
Website: --
Hours: Mon - Fri (5:30pm-7am);
Weekends from Sat (noon) -
Mon (7am)

MAINE

Brewer - *Penobscot County*
Eastern Maine Emergency
   Veterinary Clinic
15 Dirigo Drive
Brewer, ME 04412
Phone: (207) 989-6267
Fax: (207) 989-6286
Website: --
Hours: Mon - Thurs (5:30pm-8am);
      Weekends from Fri (5:30pm) -
      Mon (8am); Holidays

Lewiston - *Androscoggin County*
Animal Emergency Clinic of
   Mid-Maine
47 Strawberry Avenue
Lewiston, ME 04240
Phone: (207) 777-1110
Fax: --
Website: www.aec-midmaine.com
Hours: Nights (5pm-8am);
      Weekends & Holidays 24 hrs

Portland - *Cumberland County*
The Animal Emergency Clinic
352 Warren Avenue
Portland, ME 04103
Phone: (207) 878-3121
Fax: --
Website: --
Hours: 24 hours a day;
      7 days a week;
      365 days a year

Cee-Cee

MARYLAND

Annapolis - *Anne Arundel County*
Anne Arundel Veterinary Emergency
  Clinic, Inc. (AAVEC)
808 Bestgate Road
Annapolis, MD 21401
Phone: (410) 224-0331
Fax: (410) 573-9364
Website: www.aavec.com
Hours: 24 hours a day

Baltimore - *Baltimore City*
Falls Road Animal Hospital
6314 Falls Road
Baltimore, MD 21209
Phone: (410) 825-9100
Fax: (410) 321-6920
Website: www.fallsroad.com
Hours: 24 hours a day

Ruby

Bel Air - *Harford County*
Harford Emergency
526 Underwood Lane
Bel Air, MD 21014
Phone: (410) 420-8000
Fax: --
Website: --
Hours: 24 hours a day

Catonsville - *Baltimore County*
Emergency Veterinary Clinic
32 Mellor Avenue
Catonsville, MD 21228
Phone: (410) 792-8012
Fax: --
Website: --
Hours: Mon - Fri (6pm-8am);
         Sat & Sun & Holidays - 24 hrs

Ellicott City - *Howard County*
Emergency Animal Hospital
10270 Baltimore National Pike
  (Route 40)
Ellicott City, MD 21784
Phone: (410) 750-1177
Fax: --
Website:
  www.ellicottcityemergencyvet.com
Hours: Mon - Thurs (7pm-8am);
         Weekends from Fri (7pm) -
         Mon (8am); Holidays

Frederick - *Frederick County*
Fredrick Emergency Animal Hospital
434 Prospect Avenue
Frederick, MD 21701
Phone: (301) 662-6622
Fax: --
Website:
  www.frederickemergencyvet.com
Hours: Mon - Fri (7pm-8am);
         Sat & Sun - 24 hours

Gaithersburg - *Montgomery County*
VCA Veterinary Referral
  Association, Inc.
15021 Dufief Mill Road
Gaithersburg, MD 20878
Phone: (301) 340-3224
Fax: --
Website: www.vcavra.com
Hours: 24 hours a day; 7 days a week

(Maryland continues)

MARYLAND (continued)

Glenn Dale - *Prince George's County*
Beltway Emergency Animal Hospital
11660 Annapolis Road (Route 45)
Glenn Dale, MD 20769
Phone: (301) 464-3737
Fax: --
Website: --
Hours: Mon - Fri (8pm-8am);
    Weekends from Sat (noon) -
    Mon (8am); Holidays

Hyattstown - *Montgomery County*
Emergency Animal Center
1896 Urbana Pike (Route 355)
Hyattstown, MD 20871
Phone: (301) 831-1088
Fax: --
Website:
    www.emergencyanimalcenter.com
Hours: Nights; Weekends; Holidays

Rockville - *Montgomery County*
Metropolitan Emergency Animal Clinic
12106 Nebel Street
Rockville, MD 20852
Phone: (301) 770-5225
Fax: (301) 770-2837
Website: www.metroeac.com
Hours: Mon - Fri (6pm-8am);
    Weekends & Holidays 24 hrs

Salisbury - *Wicomico County*
Pets ER
329 Tilghman Road
Salisbury, MD 21804
Phone: (410) 543-8400
Fax: --
Website: --
Hours: Mon - Thurs (6pm-8am);
    Weekends from Fri (6pm) -
    Mon (8am)

Urbana - *Frederick County*
Greenbriar Pet Resort &
    Veterinary Center
3051 Thurston Road
Urbana, MD 21704
Phone: (301) 874-8880
Toll Free: (800) 889-9971
Fax: --
Website: www.greenbriarkennels.com
Hours: Mon - Fri (7pm-7am);
    Weekends from Sat (noon) -
    Mon (7am)

Waldorf - *Charles County*
Southern Maryland Veterinary
    Referral Center
3485 Rockefeller Court
Waldorf, MD 20602
Phone: (301) 638-0988
Fax: (301) 638-2886
Website: --
Hours: 24 hours a day;
    7 days a week;
    365 days a year

Westminster - *Carroll County*
Westminster Veterinary Hospital and
    Emergency Trauma Center
269 West Main Street
Westminster, MD 21157
Phone 1: (410) 848-3363
Phone 2: (410) 876-2717
Fax: (410) 848-4959
Website: www.24hourvethospital.com
Hours: 24 hours a day;
    7 days a week;
    365 days a year

MASSACHUSETTS

Acton - *Middlesex County*
Animal Emergency Care
164 Great Road
Acton, MA 01720
Phone: (978) 263-1742
Toll Free: (800) 454-1742
Fax: --
Website:
www.animalemergencycare.com
Hours: 24 hours a day

Boston - *Suffolk County*
Angell Animal Medical Center -
Boston Location
350 South Huntington Avenue
Boston, MA 02130
Phone: (617) 522-7282
Fax 1: (617) 522-7408
Fax 2: (617) 522-4885
Website: www.mspca.org
Hours: 24 hours a day

Buzzards Bay - *Barnstable County*
Buzzard's Bay Veterinary Associates
230 Main Street
Buzzards Bay, MA 02532
Phone: (508) 759-2521
Fax: (508) 759-6782
Website: --
Hours: Call for updated hours.
Note: Seasonal hours.

Hanover - *Plymouth County*
Roberts Animal Hospital
516 Washington Street
Hanover, MA 02339
Phone: (781) 826-2306
Fax: (781) 829-9270
Website: www.robertsanimal.com
Hours: 24 hours a day;
7 days a week;
365 days a year

Nantucket - *Nantucket County*
Angell Animal Medical Center -
Nantucket Location
21 Crooked Lane
Nantucket, MA 02554
Phone: (508) 228-1491
Fax: (508) 325-5547
Website: www.mspca.org
Hours: 24 hours a day emergency
service

North Andover - *Essex County*
Essex County Veterinary
Emergency Hospital (located at
Bulger Animal Hospital)
247 Chickering Road
North Andover, MA 01845
Phone 1: (978) 725-5544
Phone 2: (978) 682-9905
Fax: (978) 975-0133
Website: www.intownvet.com
Hours: 24 hours a day; 7 days a week

(Massachusetts continues)

Sam

MASSACHUSETTS (continued)

NORTH GRAFTON -
Worcester County
Tufts University
Cummings School of
   Veterinary Medicine
200 Westboro Road
North Grafton, MA 01536
Phone: (508) 839-5395 Main Number
Phone: (508) 839-5302
Fax: (508) 839-7951
Website: www.tufts.edu/vet
Hours: 24 hours a day, 365 days a year
   for emergencies. Call first.

Pittsfield - *Berkshire County*
Berkshire Veterinary Hospital
730 ½ Crane Avenue
Pittsfield, MA 01201
Phone: (413) 499-2820
Fax: (413) 499-7146
Website: www.berkshirevet.com
Hours: 24 hours a day

South Deerfield - *Franklin County*
Veterinary Emergency &
   Specialty Hospital
141 Greenfield Road (Routes 5/10)
South Deerfield, MA 01373
Phone: (413) 665-4911
Fax: (413) 665-4934
Website: www.veshdeerfield.com
Hours: 24 hours a day

South Dennis - *Barnstable County*
Cape Animal Referral &
   Emergency (CARE) Center
79 Theophilus Smith Road
South Dennis, MA 02660
Phone: (508) 398-7575
Toll Free: (866) 464-7575
Fax: --
Website: www.carevet.net
Hours: 24 hours a day

Springfield - *Hampden County*
Boston Road Animal Hospital
1235 Boston Road
Springfield, MA 01119
Phone: (413) 783-1203 Main
Phone: (413) 783-0603 Emergency
Fax: --
Website: www.bostonroadvets.com
Hours: 24 hours a day; 7 days a week
Note: Regular appointments
   also available.

Hannibal

Swansea - *Bristol County*
Bay State Veterinary
   Emergency Services
76 Baptist Street
Swansea, MA 02777
Phone: (508) 379-1233
Fax: --
Website: --
Hours: 24 hours a day
Note: Previously located in
   Warwick, RI.

Walpole - *Norfolk County*
TUFTS Veterinary Emergency
   Treatment Services (VETS)
525 South Street
Walpole, MA 02081
Phone: (508) 668-5454
Fax: (508) 850-9809
Website: www.tuftsvets.org
Hours: 24 hours a day

Waltham - *Middlesex County*
Veterinary Emergency Specialty Center
    of New England Animal Hospital
    (VESCONE)
180 Bear Hill Road
Waltham, MA 02454
Phone: (781) 684-8387
Fax: (781) 890-2871
Website: www.vescone.com
Hours: 24 hours a day

West Bridgewater - *Plymouth County*
Animal Emergency and
    Critical Care Center
595 West Center Street
West Bridgewater, MA 02379
Phone: (508) 580-2515
Fax: --
Website: www.neamc.com
Hours: 24 hours a day

Weymouth - *Norfolk County*
VCA South Shore Animal Hospital
595 Columbian Street
Weymouth, MA 02190
Phone: (781) 337-6622
Fax: (781) 337-0069
Website: www.vcasouthshore.com
Hours: 24 hours a day; 7 days a week

Woburn - *Middlesex County*
Massachusetts Veterinary
    Referral Hospital
21 Cabot Road
Woburn, MA 01801
Phone: (781) 932-5802
Fax: (781) 932-5837
Website: www.intownvet.com
Hours: 24 hours a day

Soda

MICHIGAN

Ann Arbor - *Washtenaw County*
Animal Emergency Clinic
4126 Packard Road
Ann Arbor, MI 48016
Phone: (734) 971-8774
Fax: --
Website: www.aecannarbor.com
Hours: 24 hours a day; 7 days a week

Ann Arbor Animal Hospital
2150 West Liberty Street
Ann Arbor, MI 48103
Phone: (734) 662-4474
Fax: (734) 662-4481
Website:
    www.annarboranimalhospital.com
Hours: 24 hours a day; 7 days a week

Auburn Hills - *Oakland County*
Michigan Veterinary Specialists -
    Auburn Hills Location
3412 East Walton Boulevard
Auburn Hills, MI 48326
Phone: (248) 371-3713
Fax: (248) 371-3714
Website: www.michvet.com
Hours: 24 hours a day; 7 days a week

Bloomfield Hills - *Oakland County*
Oakland Veterinary Referral Services
    (OVRS)
1400 South Telegraph Road
Bloomfield Hills, MI 48302
Phone: (248) 334-6877
Toll Free: (866) 334-6877
Fax: (248) 334-3693
Website: www.ovrs.com
Hours: 24 hours a day; 7 days a week

Oscar

Brighton - *Livingston County*
Town & Country Animal Hospital
4343 South Old US Highway 23
Brighton, MI 48114
Phone: (810) 220-1079
Fax: --
Website: www.24-7vet.net
Hours: 24 hours a day; 7 days a week
Note: Regular appointments
    also available.

Clinton Township - *Macomb County*
Animal Emergency Hospital
43731 Gratiot Avenue
Clinton Township, MI 48036
Phone: (586) 307-3730
Fax: --
Website:
    www.animalemergencyhospital.net
Hours: Mon - Thurs (6pm-9am);
    Weekends from Fri (6pm) -
    Mon (9am); Holidays

Detroit - *Wayne County*
Animal Emergency Room
24429 Grand River Avenue
Detroit, MI 48219
Phone: (313) 255-2404
Fax: --
Website: --
Hours: Call for updated
    emergency hours.

EAST LANSING - *Ingham County*
Michigan State University
College of Veterinary Medicine
Veterinary Medical Center
 Small Animal Clinic
East Lansing, MI 48824
Phone: (517) 353-4523
 Small Animal Appointments
Phone: (517) 353-5420
 Small Animal Emergency
Phone: (517) 353-9710
 Large Animal Emergency
Fax: (517) 432-4091
 Small Animal Office Fax
Website: www.cvm.msu.edu
Hours: 24 hours a day;
 365 days a year. Please call.

Flint - *Genesee County*
Animal Emergency Hospital of Flint
1007 South Ballenger Highway
Flint, MI 48532
Phone: (810) 238-7557
Fax: (810) 238-8027
Website:
 www.animalemergencyhospital.net
Hours: Mon - Thurs (6pm-9am);
 Weekends from Fri (6pm) -
 Mon (9am); Holidays

Grand Rapids - *Kent County*
Animal Emergency Hospital
3260 Plainfield Avenue NE
Grand Rapids, MI 49525
Phone: (616) 361-9911
Fax: (616) 225-8242
Website: --
Hours: 24 hours a day; 7 days a week;
 365 days a year

Harper Woods - *Wayne County*
East Suburbs Pet Emergency
20112 Harper Avenue
Harper Woods, MI 48225
Phone: (313) 881-6200
Fax: --
Website: --
Hours: Mon - Fri (6pm-9am);
 Weekends from Sat (1pm) -
 Mon (9am)

Kalamazoo - *Kalamazoo County*
Southwest Michigan Animal
 Emergency Hospital
3301 South Burdick
Kalamazoo, MI 49001
Phone: (269) 381-5228
Fax: (269) 381-5229
Website: --
Hours: 24 hours a day; 7 days a week

Lansing - *Ingham County*
Lansing Veterinary Urgent Care
3276 East Jolly Road
Lansing, MI 48910
Phone: (517) 393-9200
Fax: --
Website:
www.lansingveterinaryurgentcare.com
Hours: Mon - Thurs (6pm-8am);
 Weekends from Fri (6pm) -
 Mon (8am); Holidays

Madison Heights - *Oakland County*
Veterinary Emergency Service East
28223 John R Road
Madison Heights, MI 48071
Phone: (248) 547-4677 MUST CALL FIRST
Fax: --
Website: --
Hours: 24 hours a day; 7 days a week

(Michigan continues)

MICHIGAN (continued)

Milford - *Oakland County*
Veterinary Care Specialists
205 Rowe Road
Milford, MI 48380
Phone: (248) 684-0468
Fax: (248) 684-8122
Website: www.vcsmilford.com
Hours: 24 hours a day; 7 days a week

Novi - *Oakland County*
Animal Emergency Center -
  Novi Location
24255 Novi Road
Novi, MI 48375
Phone: (248) 348-1788
Fax: (248) 348-1784
Website:
  www.theanimalemergencycenter.com
Hours: 24 hours a day; 7 days a week

Q-Tip

Plymouth - *Wayne County*
Veterinary Emergency Service West
40850 Ann Arbor Road
Plymouth, MI 48170
Phone: (734) 207-8500
Fax: --
Website: --
Hours: Nights; Weekends; Holidays

Rochester - *Oakland County*
Animal Emergency Center Rochester -
  Rochester Location
265 East 2nd Street
Rochester, MI 48307
Phone: (248) 651-1788
Fax: --
Website:
  www.theanimalemergencycenter.com
Hours: Mon - Thurs (6pm-8am);
       Weekends from Fri (6pm) -
       Mon (8am)

Southfield - *Oakland County*
Michigan Veterinary Specialists -
  Southfield Location
29080 Inkster Road
Southfield, MI 48034
Phone: (248) 354-6660
Fax: (248) 354-0303
Website: www.michvet.com
Hours: 24 hours a day; 7 days a week

Southgate - *Wayne County*
Affiliated Veterinary Emergency Clinic
14085 Northline Road
Southgate, MI 48195
Phone: (734) 284-1700
Fax: (734) 284-7990
Website: www.affiliatedvet.com
Hours: Weeknights (5pm-8am);
       Weekends from Sat (noon) -
       Mon (8am); Holidays

MINNESOTA

Apple Valley - *Dakota County*
Southern Metro Animal
 Emergency Care
14690 Pennock Avenue
Apple Valley, MN 55124
Phone: (952) 953-3737
Fax: (952) 953-4453
Website: www.smaec.com
Hours: Mon - Thurs (6pm-8am);
 Weekends from Fri (6pm) -
 Mon (8am); Holidays

Coon Rapids - *Anoka County*
Affiliated Emergency Veterinary
 Services - Coon Rapids Location
1615 Coon Rapids Boulevard
Coon Rapids, MN 55433
Phone: (763) 754-9434
Fax: (763) 754-5731
Website: www.aevs.com
Hours: Mon - Thurs (6pm-8am);
 Weekends from Fri (6pm) -
 Mon (8am); Holidays

Tweety

Duluth - *St. Louis County*
Affiliated Emergency Veterinary
 Services - Duluth Location
2314 West Michigan Street
Duluth, MN 55806
Phone: (218) 302-8000
Fax: --
Website: www.aevs.com
Hours: Mon - Thurs (5pm-8am);
 Weekends from Fri (5pm) -
 Mon (8am); Holidays

Eden Prairie - *Hennepin County*
Affiliated Emergency Veterinary
 Service - Eden Prairie Location
7717 Flying Cloud Drive
Eden Prairie, MN 55344
Phone: (952) 942-8272
Fax 1: (952) 829-4089
Fax 2: (952) 233-0400
Website: www.aevs.com
Hours: 24 hours a day; 7 days a week;
 365 days a year

Gus

Golden Valley - *Hennepin County*
Affiliated Emergency Veterinary
 Service - Golden Valley Location
4708 Highway 55
Golden Valley, MN 55422
Phone: (763) 529-6560
Fax: (763) 529-1667
Website: www.aevs.com
Hours: Mon - Thurs (6pm-8am);
 Weekends from Fri (6pm) -
 Mon (8am); Holidays

Oakdale - *Washington County*
Animal Emergency Clinic
7166 10th Street North
Oakdale, MN 55128
Phone: (651) 501-3766
Fax: (651) 501-3843
Website: www.aec-tc.com
Hours: Mon - Thurs (6pm-8am);
 Weekends from Fri (6pm) -
 Mon (8am); Holidays

(Minnesota continues)

MINNESOTA (continued)

Rochester - *Olmsted County*
Affiliated Emergency Veterinary
Service - Rochester Location
121 23rd Avenue SW
Rochester, MN 55902
Phone: (507) 424-3976
Fax: --
Website: www.aevs.com
Hours: Mon - Thurs (6pm-8am);
Weekends from Fri (5pm) -
Mon (8am); Holidays

St. Cloud - *Stearns County*
Affiliated Emergency Veterinary
Service - St. Cloud Location
4180 Thielman Lane
St. Cloud, MN 56301
Phone: (320) 258-3481
Fax: (320) 258-3482
Website: www.aevs.com
Hours: Mon - Thurs (6pm-8am);
Weekends from Fri (6pm) -
Mon (8am); Holidays

SAINT PAUL - *Ramsey County*
University of Minnesota
Veterinary Medical Center
1365 Gortner Avenue
St. Paul, MN 55108
Phone: (612) 626-VETS (8387)
Small Animal Hospital
Phone: (612) 625-6700
Large Animal Hospital
Website: www.cvm.umn.edu
Hours: Emergency and patient care is
available 24 hours a day;
7 days a week.

Saint Paul - *Ramsey County*
Animal Emergency Clinic
301 University Avenue
Saint Paul, MN 55103
Phone: (651) 293-1800
Fax: (651) 291-1337
Website: www.aec-tc.com
Hours: Mon - Thurs (6pm-8am);
Weekends from Fri (6pm) -
Mon (8am); Holidays

Quincy and T.T.

MISSISSIPPI

Biloxi - *Harrison County*
Gulf Coast Veterinary
   Emergency Hospital PA
13095 Highway 67
Biloxi, MS 39532
Phone: (228) 392-7474
Fax: --
Website: --
Hours: Mon - Thurs (5pm-8am);
       Weekends from Fri (5pm) -
       Mon (8am)

Jackson - *Hinds County*
Animal Emergency Clinic
607 Monroe Street
Jackson, MS 39202
Phone: (601) 352-8383
Fax: --
Website: --
Hours: Nights; Weekends;
       Holidays - Call.

Hattiesburg - *Forrest County*
Animal ER (located at
   Animal Medical Center)
3422 Hardy Street
Hattiesburg, MS 39402
Phone: (601) 264-5785
Fax: --
Website: www.animal-er.com
Hours: 24 hours a day; 7 days a week

Emergency Vets
6447 US Highway 49
Hattiesburg, MS 39401
Phone: (601) 450-3838
Fax: --
Website: --
Hours: Mon - Fri (6pm-8am);
       Weekends from Sat (noon) -
       Mon (8am)

Roxy

Horn Lake - *DeSoto County*
Horn Lake Animal Hospital, Inc.
3390 Goodman Road West
Horn Lake, MS 38637
Phone: (662) 393-1116
Fax: (662) 393-8246
Website: www.hornlakeanimal.com
Hours: 24 hours a day; 7 days a week

MISSISSIPPI STATE -
  Oktibbeha County
Mississippi State University
Mississippi State, MS 39762
Phone: (662) 325-1351 Appointments
Phone: (662) 325-3432 Emergencies
Fax: (662) 325-4596
Website: www.cvm.msstate.edu
Hours: Emergency and patient care
       is available 24 hours a day;
       7 days a week.

MISSOURI

Barnhart - *Jefferson County*
Animal Emergency Clinic Jefferson Co.
7095 Metropolitan - Suite 6
Barnhart, MO 63012
Phone: (636) 464-2846
Fax: (636) 467-5701
Website: --
Hours: Mon - Thurs (6pm-8am);
Weekends from Fri (6pm) -
Mon (8am); Holidays

Belton - *Cass County*
Animal Urgent Care of Cass County
(located at Belton Animal Clinic)
1308 North Scott Avenue
Belton, MO 64012
Phone: (816) 331-3120
Fax: (816) 322-7377
Website: www.beltonanimal.com
Hours: Weeknights (6pm-1pm);
Weekends and Holidays
Note: Daytime practice also at
this location.

Bridgeton - *St. Louis County*
Animal Emergency Clinic North
12501 Natural Bridge
Bridgeton, MO 63044
Phone: (314) 739-1500
Fax: (314) 739-7977
Website: --
Hours: Mon - Thurs (6pm-8am);
Weekends from Fri (6pm) -
Mon (8am); Holidays

COLUMBIA - *Boone County*
University of Missouri
College of Veterinary Medicine
379 East Campus Drive
Columbia, MO 65211
Phone: (573) 882-7821 Appointments
Phone: (573) 882-4589 Emergency
Fax: (573) 884-5444
Website: www.vmth.missouri.edu
Hours: 24 hours a day; 7 days a week.
Note: Regular appointments
also available.

Avis (with Grammy)

Kansas City - *Jackson County*
Animal Emergency Center
8141 North Oak Trfy
Kansas City, MO 64118
Phone: (816) 455-5430
Fax: (816) 455-5602
Website: --
Hours: Mon - Fri (6pm-7:30am);
Weekends from Sat (noon) -
Mon (7:30am); Holidays

Lees Summit - *Jackson County*
Animal Emergency & Referral Hospital
3495 Northeast Ralph Powell Road
Lees Summit, MO 64064
Phone: (816) 554-4990
Fax: (816) 524-2973
Website: --
Hours: Mon - Fri (6pm-8am);
Weekends from Sat (6am) -
Mon (8am); Holidays

O'Fallon - *St. Charles County*
Animal Emergency Clinic
334 Fort Zumwalt Square
O'Fallon, MO 63366
Phone: (636) 240-5496
Fax: (636) 980-1467
Website: --
Hours: Mon - Thurs (6pm-8am);
Weekends from Fri (6pm) -
Mon (8am)

St. Louis - *St. Louis County*
Animal Emergency Clinic South
9937 Big Bend Boulevard
St. Louis, MO 63122
Phone: (314) 822-7600
Fax: (314) 822-5348
Website: --
Hours: 24 hours a day;
7 days a week

Springfield - *Greene County*
Emergency Veterinary Clinic of
Southwest Missouri
400 South Glenstone Avenue
Springfield, MO 65802
Phone: (417) 890-1600
Fax: --
Website: --
Hours: Mon - Fri (6pm-8am);
Weekends from Sat (8am) -
Mon (8am); Holidays

Hercules

MONTANA

Billings - *Yellowstone County*
Best Friend's Animal Hospital &
   Urgent Care Center
1530 Popelka Drive
Billings, MT 59105
Phone: (406) 255-0500
Fax: (406) 255-0510
Website: www.bestfriendsvetcare.com
Hours: 24 hours a day

Columbia Falls - *Flathead County*
Grizzly Moon Mobile Animal Service
PO Box 597
Columbia Falls, MT 59912
Phone: (406) 892-4749
Fax: --
Website: --
Hours: Call.

Missoula - *Missoula County*
Western Montana Small Animal
   Emergency Clinic
1914 South Reserve Street
Missoula, MT 59801
Phone: (406) 829-9300
Fax: --
Website: --
Hours: Mon - Thurs (5:30pm-8am);
      Weekends from Fri (5:30pm) -
      Mon (8am); Holidays

Max

NEBRASKA

Lincoln - *Lancaster County*
Veterinary Emergency
  Treatment Services
2540 South 48th Street
Lincoln, NE 68506
Phone: (402) 489-6800
Fax: (402) 489-6826
Website: www.uvets.com
Hours: Mon - Fri (6pm-7am);
        Weekends from Sat (noon) -
        Mon (7am); Holidays

Omaha - *Douglas County*
Animal Emergency Clinic, P.C. -
  West Dodge Road Location
15791 West Dodge Road
Omaha, NE 68118
Phone: (402) 504-1731
Fax: --
Website: www.eclinicomaha.com
Hours: Nights; Weekends; Holidays
Note: Please call before coming in.

Animal Emergency Clinic, P.C. -
  Mockingbird Drive Location
9664 Mockingbird Drive
Omaha NE 68127
Phone: (402) 339-6232
Fax: --
Website: www.eclinicomaha.com
Hours: Mon - Thurs (6pm-8am);
        Weekends from Fri (6pm) -
        Mon (8am); Holidays
Note: Please call before coming in.

Rosey

NEVADA

Carson City - *Carson City County*
Carson Tahoe Veterinary Hospital
3389 South Carson Street
Carson City, NV 89701
Phone: (775) 883-8238
Fax: (775) 883-8275
Website: --
Hours: 24 hours a day;
      7 days a week;
      365 days a year
Note: Daytime practice also at
      this location.

Las Vegas - *Clark County*
Animal Emergency Center
3340 East Patrick Lane
Las Vegas, NV 89120
Phone: (702) 457-8050
Fax: --
Website: --
Hours: Mon - Thurs (6pm-8am);
      Weekends from Fri (6pm) -
      Mon (8am)

East Charleston 24 hour
   Animal Hospital
701 East Charleston Boulevard
Las Vegas, NV 89104
Phone: (702) 386-0901
Fax: (702) 382-0901
Website: --
Hours: 24 hours a day; 7 days a week

Las Vegas Animal Emergency Hospital
5231 West Charleston Boulevard
Las Vegas, NV 89146
Phone: (702) 822-1045
Fax: --
Website: www.lvaeh.com
Hours: Mon - Thurs (6pm-8am);
      Weekends from Fri (6pm) -
      Mon (8am); Holidays

West Flamingo Animal Hospital
5445 West Flamingo Road
Las Vegas, NV 89103
Phone: (702) 876-2111
Fax: --
Website: --
Hours: 24 hours a day

Reno - *Washoe County*
Animal Emergency Center
6425 South Virginia Street
Reno, NV 89511
Phone: (775) 851-3600
Fax: --
Website: --
Hours: Mon - Fri (6pm-8am);
      Weekends from Sat (8pm) -
      Mon (8am); Holidays

Cosmo

NEW HAMPSHIRE

Brentwood - *Rockingham County*
Veterinary Emergency and
   Surgery Hospital of Brentwood
168 Crawley Falls Road (Located on
Highway 125)
Brentwood, NH 03833
Phone: (603) 642-9111
Fax: (603) 642-9115
Website: www.veshnh.com
Hours: 24 hours a day; 7 days a week

Concord - *Merrimack County*
Capital Area Veterinary
   Emergency Services (CAVES)
Ralph Pill Building
22 Bridge Street
Concord, NH 03301
Phone: (603) 227-1199
Toll Free: (877) 929-1199
Fax: (603) 227-0666
Website: www.capareaves.org
Hours: 24 hours a day; 7 days a week

Manchester - *Hillsborough County*
Veterinary Emergency Center of
   Manchester
55 Carl Drive
Manchester, NH 03103
Phone: (603) 666-6677
Toll Free: (800) 974-6688
Fax: --
Website: --
Hours: 24 hours a day; 7 days a week

Nashua - *Hillsborough County*
The Animal Medical Center of
   New England
168 Main Dunstable Road
Nashua, NH 03060
Phone: (603) 821-7222
Fax: (603) 821-7221
Website: www.amcne.com
Hours: 24 hours a day; 7 days a week

Portsmouth - *Rockingham County*
Emergency Veterinary Clinic of
   the Seacoast Region
300 Gosling Road
Portsmouth, NH 03801
Phone: (603) 431-3600
Fax: (603) 431-1751
Website: www.seacoastevc.com
Hours: 24 hours a day;
      7 days a week;
      365 days a year

Snickers
(in good
hands!)

NEW JERSEY

Clarksburg - *Monmouth County*
Veterinary Surgical &
  Diagnostic Specialists
34 Trenton Lakewood Road
Clarksburg, NJ 08510
Phone: (609) 259-8300
Fax: (609) 259-8484
Website: www.vsds.net
Hours: 24 hours a day;
  7 days a week;
  365 days a year

Fairfield - *Essex County*
Animal Emergency and
  Referral Associates
1237 Bloomfield Avenue
Fairfield, NJ 07004
Phone 1: (973) 226-3282
Phone 2: (973) 788-0500
Fax: (973) 788-0502
Website: www.animalerc.com
Hours: Mon - Thurs (5pm-8am);
  Weekends from Fri (8am) -
  Mon (8am); Holidays

Iselin - *Middlesex County*
Central Jersey Veterinary
  Emergency Service
643 Lincoln Highway
Iselin, NJ 08830
Phone: (732) 283-3535
Fax: --
Website: www.cjemergencyvet.com
Hours: Mon - Fri (8pm-8am);
  Weekends from Sat (1pm) -
  Mon (8am)

Lakewood - *Ocean County*
Jersey Shore Veterinary
  Emergency Service
1000 State Highway North 70
Lakewood, NJ 08701
Phone: (732) 363-3200
Fax: --
Website: --
Hours: Mon - Fri (8pm-8am);
  Weekends from Sat (3pm) -
  Mon (8am)

Linwood - *Atlantic County*
South Jersey Veterinary
  Emergency Service
535 Maple Avenue
Linwood, NJ 08221
Phone: (609) 926-5300
Fax: (609) 926-5799
Website: www.sjves.net
Hours: 24 hours a day; 7 days a week;
  365 days a year

Lyndhurst - *Bergen County*
North Jersey Veterinary
  Emergency Services (NJVES)
724 Ridge Road
Lyndhurst, NJ 07071
Phone: (201) 438-7122
Fax: (201) 438-7124
Website: www.njves.com
Hours: Mon - Fri (6pm-7:30am);
  Weekends from Sat (noon) -
  Mon (7:30am)

Claudette

Mount Laurel - *Burlington County*
Animal Emergency Service of
  South Jersey
220 Moorestown - Mt. Laurel Road
Mount Laurel, NJ 08054
Phone: (856) 727-1332
Fax: (856) 234-7626
Website: www.aessj.com
Hours: Mon - Fri (8pm-8am);
        Weekends from Sat (noon) -
        Mon (8am); Holidays

Newton - *Sussex County*
Newton Veterinary Hospital
116 Hampton House Road (Route 206)
Newton, NJ 07860
Phone: (973) 383-4321
Fax: (973) 383-7544
Website: www.newtonvet.com
Hours: 24 hours a day; 7 days a week;
       365 days a year
Note: Regular appointments
      also available.

Paramus - *Bergen County*
Oradell Animal Hospital, Inc.
580 Winters Avenue
Paramus, NJ 07652
Phone: (201) 262-0010
Toll Free: (800) 624-1883
Fax: (201) 262-4275
Website: www.oradell.com
Hours: 24 hours a day; 7 days a week

Randolph - *Morris County*
Alliance Emergency Veterinary Clinic
540 Route 10 West
Randolph, NJ 07869
Phone: (973) 328-2844
Fax: (973) 328-8553
Website: --
Hours: Mon - Fri (8pm-8am);
        Weekends from Sat (noon) -
        Mon (8am); Holidays

Blue

Raritan - *Somerset County*
Animerge
21 US Highway 206
Raritan, NJ 08869
Phone: (908) 707-9077
Fax: --
Website: www.animerge.net
Hours: 24 hours a day; 7 days a week;
       365 days a year

Succasunna - *Morris County*
Alliance Emergency Veterinary Clinic
275 State Route 10 East - Suites 220-40
Succasunna, NJ 07876
Phone: (973) 328-2844
Fax: --
Website: --
Hours: Weeknights (8pm-8am);
        Weekends & Major Holidays -
        24 hours

(New Jersey continues)

NEW JERSEY (continued)

Tinton Falls - *Monmouth County*
Garden State Veterinary Specialists
One Pine Street
Tinton Falls, NJ 07753
Phone: (732) 922-0011
Fax: (732) 922-0991
Website: www.gsvs.org
Hours: 24 hours a day; 7 days a week

Red Bank Veterinary Hospital
197 Hance Avenue
Tinton Falls, NJ 07724
Phone: (732) 747-3636
Fax: (732) 747-6562
Website: www.rbvh.net
Hours: 24 hours a day; 7 days a week

Union City - *Hudson County*
Ambassador Veterinary Hospital
3714 Kennedy Boulevard
Union City, NJ 07087
Phone: (201) 863-4072
Fax: (201) 902-1373
Website: www.avhnj.com
Hours: 24-Hour Emergency Service
must phone (201) 863-4072

Jethro

NEW MEXICO

Albuquerque - *Bernalillo County*
Veterinary Emergency &
  Specialty Center of New Mexico
4000 Montgomery Boulevard NE
Albuquerque, NM 87109
Phone: (505) 884-3433
Fax: (505) 884-6679
Website: www.vetspecialistofnm.com
Hours: 24 hours a day; 7 days a week

Albuquerque Westside
  Animal Emergency Clinic
6633 Caminito Coors NW
Albuquerque, NM 87120-3120
Phone: (505) 898-8874
Fax: --
Website: --
Hours: Call for updated
         emergency hours.

VCA Veterinary Care Animal Hospital
9901 Montgomery Boulevard
Albuquerque, NM 87111
Phone: (505) 292-5353
Fax: (505) 293-9402
Website: www.vcavetcare.com
Hours: Sun - Sat (7am-11pm); Call
Note: 24 hour care

Lola

Las Cruces - *Dona Ana County*
Veterinary Emergency Services
162 Wyatt Drive
Las Cruces, NM 88005
Phone: (505) 527-8100
Fax: --
Website: --
Hours: Mon - Fri (6pm-8am);
         Weekends from Sat (noon) -
         Mon (8am)

Los Lunas - *Valencia County*
Pet ER
335 Highway 314 SW
Los Lunas, NM 87031
Phone: (505) 565-3737
Fax: --
Website: --
Hours: Mon - Thurs (6pm-8am);
         Weekends from Fri (6pm) -
         Mon (8am)

Santa Fe - *Santa Fe County*
Emergency Veterinary Clinic of
  Santa Fe
1311 Calle Mava
Santa Fe, NM 87505
Phone: (505) 984-0625
Fax: (505) 984-8705
Website: --
Hours: Mon - Thurs (5pm-8am);
         Weekends from Fri (5pm) -
         Mon (8am)

NEW YORK

Baldwinsville - *Onondaga County*
Veterinary Emergency &
   Critical Care Center
2115 Downer Street Road
Baldwinsville, NY 13027
Phone: (315) 638-3500
Fax: (315) 638-3647
Website: www.veccc.com
Hours: Mon - Thurs (7pm-8am);
      Weekends from Fri (7pm) -
      Mon (8am); Holidays

Ballston Lake - *Saratoga County*
Northway Animal Emergency Clinic
Northway (Exit 17 North)
Ballston Lake, NY 12019
Phone: (518) 761-2602
Fax: --
Website: --
Hours: Mon - Fri (6pm-8am);
      Weekends - Call

Bedford Hills - *Westchester County*
Katonah Bedford Veterinary Center
546 North Bedford Road (Route 117)
Bedford Hills, NY 10507
Phone: (914) 241-7700
Fax: (914) 241-7708
Website: www.kbvetcenter.com
Hours: 24 hours a day;
      7 days a week;
      365 days a year

Bohemia - *Suffolk County*
Atlantic Coast Veterinary Specialists
3250 Veterans Memorial Highway
Bohemia, NY 11716
Phone: (631) 285-7780
Fax: --
Website: --
Hours: 24 hours a day;
      7 days a week

Brooklyn - *Kings County*
Veterinary Emergency &
   Referral Group (VERG)
318 Warren Street
Brooklyn, NY 11201
Phone: (718) 522-9400
Fax: (718) 522-9755
Website: www.vetemergencygroup.com
Hours: 24 hours a day;
      7 days a week;
      365 days a year

Buffalo - *Erie County*
Animal Emergency Care
4949 Main Street
Buffalo, NY 14226
Phone: (716) 839-4043
Fax: --
Website:
 www.greaterbuffaloemergencyvet.com
Hours: Mon - Thurs (6pm-9am);
      Weekends from Fri -
      Mon 24 hours; Holidays

Paris

Commack - *Suffolk County*
Animal Emergency Service
6230-C Jericho Turnpike
Commack, NY 11725
Phone: (631) 462-6044
Fax: --
Website:
   www.animalemergencysvce.com
Hours: Mon - Thurs (5pm-9am);
      Weekends from Fri (5pm) -
      Mon (9am); Holidays

Farmingdale - *Nassau County*
Animal Emergency Service (located at
    New York Specialty Clinic)
2233 Broadhollow Road
Farmingdale, NY 11735
Phone: (631) 249-2899 Emergency
Phone: (631) 694-3400 Clinic
Fax: (631) 694-3401 Clinic
Website:
    www.animalemergencysvce.com
    (Emergency)
Website: www.nyvsc.com (Clinic)
Hours: 24 hours a day; 7 days a week

Flushing - *Queens County*
A Elmhurst Animal Emergency
8706 Queens Boulevard
Flushing, NY 11373
Phone: (718) 426-4444
Fax: (718) 426-3611
Website: www.drkonstalid.com
Hours: Mon - Thurs (5pm-8am);
        Weekends from Fri (5pm) -
        Mon (8am); Holidays

Gansevoort - *Saratoga County*
Northway Animal Emergency
35 Fawn Road
Gansevoort, NY 12831
Phone: (518) 761-2602
Fax: (518) 798-0692
Website: --
Hours: Mon - Fri (6pm-8am);
        Weekends - Call

Grand Island - *Erie County*
Grand Island Small Animal Hospital
2323 Whitehaven Road
Grand Island, NY 14072
Phone: (716) 773-7646
Fax: (716) 774-8234
Website: www.gianimalhospital.com
Hours: 24 hours a day

Buddy

Greenvale - *Nassau County*
Roslyn Veterinary Group
1 Northern Boulevard
Greenvale, NY 11548
Phone: (516) 621-1744
Fax: (516) 621-8663
Website:
    www.roslynveterinarygroup.com
Hours: Mon - Sun - 24 Hour Service

Huntington - *Suffolk County*
West Hills Animal Hospital
800 West Jericho Turnpike
Huntington, NY 11743
Phone: (631) 351-6116
Fax: (631) 367-8130
Website: www.whahzoo.vetsuite.com
Hours: 24 hours a day; 7 days a week

(New York continues)

NEW YORK (continued)

ITHACA - *Tompkins County*
Cornell University
College of Veterinary Medicine
Ithaca, NY 14853
Phone: (607) 253-3060
   Small Animal Emergency
Phone: (607) 253-3100
   Large Animal Emergency
Fax: --
Website: www.vet.cornell.edu
Hours: Emergency services available
     24 hours a day;
     7 days a week
Note: Regular appointments
     also available.

Jamaica - *Queens County*
Animal Emergency Center of Queens
18711 Hillside Avenue
Jamaica, NY 11432
Phone: (718) 454-4141
Fax: --
Website: --
Hours: Call for updated
     emergency hours.

Kingston - *Ulster County*
Animal Emergency Clinic of
   The Hudson Valley
1112 Morton Boulevard
Kingston, NY 12401
Phone: (845) 336-0713
Fax: --
Website: --
Hours: Mon - Thurs (6pm-8am);
     Weekends from Fri (6pm) -
     Mon (8am); Holidays

Latham - *Albany County*
Capital District Animal
   Emergency Clinic
222 Troy Schenectady Road
Latham, NY 12110
Phone: (518) 785-1094
Fax: (518) 785-5363
Website: --
Hours: Mon - Fri (5pm-8am);
     Sat & Sun & Holidays - 24 hrs

Middletown - *Orange County*
Emergency Orange County
   Animal Service
517 Route 211 East
Middletown, NY 10940
Phone: (845) 692-0260
Fax: (845) 692-3563
Website: www.animalemergencyoc.com
Hours: Mon - Thurs (5pm-8am);
     Weekends from Fri (5pm) -
     Mon (8am); Holidays

New York - *New York County*
Fifth Avenue Veterinary Specialists
1 West 15th Street
New York, NY 10011
Phone: (212) 924-3311
Fax: (212) 924-7228
Website: www.5thavevetspecialist.com
Hours: 24-hour staffing:
     24 hours a day; 7 days a week;
     365 days a year

NYC Veterinary Specialists And
   Cancer Treatment Center
410 West 55th Street
New York, NY 10019
Phone: (212) 767-0099
Fax: (212) 767-0098
Website: www.nyc-vs.com
Hours: Call for updated
     emergency hours.

Gucci

Park East Animal Hospital
52 East 64th Street
New York, NY 10021
Phone: (212) 832-8417
Fax: --
Website:
   www.parkeastanimalhospital.com
Hours: 24 hours a day; 7 days a week

The Animal Medical Center
510 East 62nd Street
New York, NY 10021
Phone: (212) 838-8100
   Main Number
Phone: (212) 838-7053
   Regular Appointments
Fax: --
Website: www.amcny.org
Hours: 24 hours a day; 7 days a week;
     365 days a year
Note: Regular appointments
     also available.

Westside Veterinary Center
220 West 83rd Street
New York, NY 10024
Phone: (212) 580-1800
Fax: (212) 362-8948
Website: www.westsidevetcenter.com
Hours: 24 hours a day staffed;
     7 days a week

**New York City Area
24 hour Emergency
Pet Transportation:**

Pet Chauffeur
Phone: (718) 752-1767

Pet Taxi
Phone: (212) 755-1757

Greater NYC area
   Ambulance Transportation
Phone: 1-800-AMBUVET
   (1-800-262-8838)
Website: www.ambuvet.com

Orchard Park - *Erie County*
Orchard Park Veterinary
   Medical Center
3507 Orchard Park Road
Orchard Park, NY 14127
Phone: (716) 662-6660
Fax: --
Website: www.opvmc.com
Hours: Mon - Fri (6pm-8am);
     Sat & Sun & Holidays - 24 hrs
Note: Daytime practice also at
     this location.

Plainview - *Nassau County*
Animal Emergency &
   Critical Care Center (located at
   Long Island Veterinary Specialists)
163 South Service Road
Plainview, NY 11803
Phone: (516) 501-1700
Fax: (516) 501-1169
Website: www.livs.org
Hours: 24 hours a day;
     7 days a week

(New York continues)

NEW YORK (continued)

Poughkeepsie - *Dutchess County*
Animal Emergency Clinic of
   Poughkeepsie
84 Patrick Lane
Noxon Business Park
Poughkeepsie, NY 12603
Phone: (845) 471-8242
Fax: --
Website: --
Hours: Mon - Thurs (6pm-8am);
      Weekends from Fri (6pm) -
      Mon (8am); Holidays

Riverhead - *Suffolk County*
East End Veterinary Emergency &
   Specialty Center
67 Commerce Drive
Riverhead, NY 11901
Phone: (631) 369-4513
Fax: --
Website: www.pet-er.com
Hours: 24 hours a day; 7 days a week

Rochester - *Monroe County*
Animal Emergency Service
825 White Spruce Boulevard
Rochester, NY 14623
Phone: (585) 424-1277
Fax: (585) 475-0437
Website:
   www.animalemergencyservices.com
Hours: 24 hours a day; 7 days a week

Selden - *Suffolk County*
Animal Emergency Service
280 Middle Country Road
Selden, NY 11784
Phone: (631) 698-2225
Fax: (631) 698-2250
Website:
   www.animalemergencysvce.com
Hours: 24 hours a day;
      7 days a week

Staten Island - *Richmond County*
Emergency Veterinarians Clinic
125 New Dorp Lane
Staten Island, NY 10306
Phone: (718) 370-1102
Fax: --
Website: --
Hours: Mon - Sat (8am-11pm);
      Sun (8am-6pm)

Veterinary Emergency Center
1293 Clove Road
Staten Island, NY 10301
Phone: (718) 720-4211
Fax: --
Website: --
Hours: Call for updated
      emergency hours.

Syracuse - *Onondaga County*
Veterinary Medical Center of
   Central New York
5841 Bridge Street - Suite 200
East Syracuse, NY 13057
Phone: (315) 446-7933
Fax: (315) 446-0920
Website: www.vmccny.com
Hours: 24 hours a day; 7 days a week

Valley Cottage - *Rockland County*
Valley Cottage Animal Hospital
202 Route 303
Valley Cottage, NY 10989
Phone: (845) 268-9263
Fax: (845) 268-0516
Website:
  www.valleycottageanimalhospital.com
Hours: 24 hours a day;
      7 days a week;
      365 days a year
Note: Daytime practice also at
      this location.

Valley Stream - *Nassau County*
Central Veterinary Associates
73 West Merrick Road
Valley Stream, NY 11580
Phone 1: (516) 825-3066
Phone 2: (718) 525-5454
Fax: (516) 561-5001
Website: www.centralvets.com
Hours: 24 hours a day

West Islip - *Suffolk County*
Veterinary Medical Center of
    Long Island
75 Sunrise Highway
West Islip, NY 11795
Phone: (631) 587-0800
Fax: (631) 587-2006
Website: www.vmcli.com
Hours: 24 hours a day

Westbury - *Nassau County*
Nassau Animal Emergency Group
740 Old Country Road
Westbury, NY 11590
Phone: (516) 333-6262
Fax: --
Website:
    www.nassauanimalemergency.com
Hours: Mon - Fri (7pm-8am);
        Weekends from Sat (1pm) -
        Mon (8am); Holidays

The Center for Specialized
    Veterinary Care
609-5 Cantiague Rock Road
Westbury, NY 11590
Phone: (516) 420-0000
Fax: (516) 420 - 0122
Website: www.vetspecialist.com
Hours: 24 hours a day; 7 days a week;
        365 days a year
Note: Pet emergency transportation
        may be available.

White Plains - *Westchester County*
Veterinary Emergency Group
193 Tarrytown Road (Route 119)
White Plains, NY 10607
Phone: (914) 949-8779
Fax: (914) 949-2393
Website:
    www.veterinaryemergencygroup.com
Hours: Weeknights (6pm-8am);
        Weekends from Fri (6pm) -
        Mon (8am); Holidays

Abby

NORTH CAROLINA

Asheville - *Buncombe County*
The Regional Emergency
   Animal Care Hospital (REACH)
677 Brevard Road
Asheville, NC 28806
Phone: (828) 665-4399
Fax: (828) 665-2629
Website: www.reach.vetsuite.com
Hours: Mon - Fri (5pm-7am);
        Sat & Sun & Holidays - 24 hrs

Boone - *Watauga County*
Animal Emergency Clinic of
   the High Country
1126 Blowing Rock Road - Suite A
Boone, NC 28607
Phone: (828) 268-2833
Fax: (828) 268-2818
Website: www.boonevet.net
Hours: Weeknights (6pm-8am);
       Weekends from Fri (6pm) -
       Mon (8am); Holidays

Burlington - *Alamance County*
Central Carolina Veterinary Hospital
1919 South Church Street
Burlington, NC 27215
Phone: (336) 229-0060
Fax: --
Website: --
Hours: 24 hours a day; 7 days a week
Note: Regular appointments
        also available.

Alamance Animal Emergency Hospital
2643 Ramada Road
Burlington, NC 27215
Phone: (336) 792-2206
Fax: --
Website: --
Hours: Mon - Fri (6pm-9am);
       Weekends from Sat (noon) -
       Mon (9am); Holidays

Cary - *Wake County*
Animal Emergency Clinic of Cary
220 High House Road - Suite 101
Cary, NC 27513
Phone: (919) 462-8989
Fax: --
Website: --
Hours: Mon - Fri (5:30pm-8am);
       Weekends from Sat (noon) -
       Mon (8am)

Veterinary Specialty Hospital
6405 Tryon Road - Suite 100
Cary, NC 27511
Phone: (919) 233-4911
Fax: (919) 854-1155
Website: www.vetspechosp.com
Hours: 24 hours a day; 7 days a week;
       365 days a year

Charleston - *Charleston County*
Greater Charleston
   Emergency Veterinary Clinic
3163 West Montague Avenue
North Charleston, SC 29418
Phone: (843) 744-3372
Fax: --
Website: --
Hours: Mon - Thurs (6pm-8am);
       Weekends from Fri (6pm) -
       Mon (8am)

Charlotte - *Mecklenburg County*
Animal Medical Hospital
3832 Monroe Road
Charlotte, NC 28205
Phone: (704) 334-4684
Fax: (704) 358-3564
Website: www.animalmedical.net
Hours: 24 hours a day; 7 days a week

Carolina Veterinary Specialists
  Medical Center
South Charlotte Medical Center
2225 Township Road
Charlotte, NC 28273
Phone: (704) 588-7015 Emergency
Phone: (704) 504-9608 Main
Fax: (704) 504-9606
Website: www.carolinavet.com
Hours: Weeknights (after 5pm);
        Weekends & Major Holidays -
        24 hours
Note: Daytime practice also at
        this location.

Andy

Durham - *Durham County*
Triangle Pet Emergency
  Treatment Service (T-PETS)
3319 Chapel Hill Boulevard
Durham, NC 27707
Phone: (919) 489-0615
Fax: --
Website: www.trianglevet.com
Hours: Mon - Thurs (6pm-8am);
        Weekends from Fri (6pm) -
        Mon (8am)

I BREAK FOR WEIMARANERS

Fayetteville - *Cumberland County*
Animal Urgent Care of Fayetteville, P.A.
3635 Sycamore Dairy Road
Fayetteville, NC 28303
Phone: (910) 864-2844
Fax: --
Website: --
Hours: Mon - Thurs (6pm-8am);
        Weekends from Fri (6pm) -
        Mon (8am)

Gastonia - *Gaston County*
Veterinary Emergency Clinic of
  Gaston County, P.A .
728 East Franklin Boulevard
Gastonia, NC 28054
Phone: (704) 866-7918
Toll Free: (800) 768-5179
Fax: --
Website: --
Hours: Mon - Fri (5:30pm-8am);
        Weekends from Sat (noon) -
        Mon (8am)

Greensboro - *Guilford County*
After Hours Veterinary
  Emergency Clinic
5505 West Friendly Avenue
Greensboro, NC 27405
Phone: (336) 851-1990
Fax: (336) 851-1993
Website: www.ahvec.com
Hours: Mon - Fri (6pm-8am);
        Weekends from Sat (noon) -
        Mon (8am); Holidays

(North Carolina continues)

NORTH CAROLINA (continued)

Carolina Veterinary Specialists
 Animal Emergency & Trauma Center
501 Nicholas Road
Greensboro, NC 27409
Phone: (336) 632-0605
Fax: --
Website: www.carolinavet.com
Hours: 24 hours a day; 7 days a week;
 365 days a year

Puff

Hickory - *Catawba County*
After Hours Emergency
 Veterinary Clinic
321 Business Park
126 Highway 321 Southwest
Hickory, NC 28602
Phone: (828) 428-0760
Fax: --
Website: --
Hours: Mon - Fri (5:30pm-8am);
 Weekends from Sat (noon) -
 Mon (8am); Holidays

Huntersville - *Mecklenburg County*
Carolina Veterinary Specialists
 Huntersville Specialty and
 Emergency Hospital
12117 Statesville Road
Huntersville, NC 28078
Phone: (704) 949-1100
Fax: (704) 949-1101
Website: www.carolinavet.com
Hours: 24 hours a day; 7 days a week;
 365 days a year
Note: Regular veterinary facility
 during the day.

Jacksonville - *Onslow County*
Coastal Veterinary Emergency Clinic
New River Shopping Center
1200 Hargett Street
Jacksonville, NC 28540
Phone: (910) 455-3838
Fax: --
Website: --
Hours: Nights; Weekends; Holidays

Kannapolis - *Cabarrus County*
Cabarrus Emergency
 Veterinarian Clinic
1317 South Cannon Boulevard
Kannapolis, NC 28083
Phone 1: (704) 932-1196
Phone 2: (704) 932-1182
Fax: --
Website: --
Hours: Mon - Thurs (5:30pm-8am);
 Weekends from Fri (5:30pm) -
 Mon (8am)

Matthews - *Mecklenburg County*
Emergency Veterinary Clinic
2440 Plantation Center Drive
Matthews, NC 28105
Phone: (704) 844-6440
Fax: (704) 844-8738
Website: --
Hours: 24 hours a day

Boo-Boo

RALEIGH - *Wake County*
North Carolina State University
Veterinary Teaching Hospital
4700 Hillsborough Street
Raleigh, NC 27606
Phone: (919) 513-6911
    Small Animal Emergency Service
Phone: (919) 513-6630 (or 6640)
    Large Animal Emergency Service
Fax: --
Website: --
Hours: Mon - Thurs (5pm-8am);
    Weekends from Fri (5pm) -
    Mon (8am); Holidays
Note: Emergencies after hours
    do not require a referral.
    Must call.

Raleigh - *Wake County*
After Hours Emergency Clinic
409 Vick Avenue
Raleigh, NC 27612
Phone: (919) 781-5145
Fax: (919) 782-7061
Website:
    www.afterhoursanimalclinic.com
Hours: Mon - Thurs (5:30pm-8am);
    Weekends from Fri (5:30pm) -
    Mon (8am); Holidays

Quail Corners Animal Hospital &
    24 Hour Emergency Care Center
1613 East Millbrook Road
Raleigh, NC 27609
Phone: (919) 876-0739
Fax: --
Website: www.quailandhiddenah.com
Hours: 24 hours a day;
    7 days a week;
    365 days a year
Note: Daytime practice also at
    this location.

Veterinary Specialty Hospital
4640 Paragon Park Road
Raleigh, NC 27616
Phone: (919) 861-0109
Fax: (919) 277-0790
Website: www.vetspechosp.com
Hours: 24 hours a day

Bitsy

Reidsville - *Rockingham County*
Reidsville Veterinary Hospital
1401 West Harrison Street
Reidsville, NC 27320
Phone: (336) 349-3194
Fax: (336) 349-8615
Website: www.reidsvillevet.com
Hours: 24 hours a day

Wilmington - *New Hanover County*
Animal Emergency Clinic of
    Wilmington
5333 Oleander Drive
Wilmington, NC 28403
Phone: (910) 791-7387
Fax: --
Website: --
Hours: Mon - Fri (6pm-8am);
    Weekends from Sat (noon) -
    Mon (8am); Holidays

(North Carolina continues)

NORTH CAROLINA (continued)

Wilson - *Wilson County*
East Carolina Veterinary
   Emergency Treatment Services
4909-D Expressway Drive
Wilson, NC 27893
Phone: (252) 265-9920
Fax: --
Website: www.ecvpetcare.com
Hours: Mon - Fri (6pm-8am);
     Weekends from Fri (6pm) -
     Mon (8am); Holidays

Winston Salem - *Forsyth County*
Animal Emergency & Trauma Center
   Forsyth Veterinary Clinic
7781 North Point Boulevard
Winston Salem, NC 27106
Phone: (336) 896-0902
Fax: (336) 896-1969
Website: --
Hours: Mon - Thurs (6pm-8am);
     Weekends from Fri (6pm) -
     Mon (8am); Holidays

Consuelo

" *Thank goodness for 24-hour pet emergency clinics. Animals can suffer injuries that require professional attention at any time, and Murphy's Law means that they often have accidents after hours, when normal veterinary clinics are closed.*

"I was very grateful for the 24-hour pet emergency clinic when my greyhound, Phoenix, hurt himself seriously on a sunny Mother's Day Sunday. He severed an artery in his front leg when he tripped on a tall sprinkler while running at full speed. Another time, because of a dog fight, one of my other dogs had his entire ear severed – again on a Sunday afternoon. Thanks to the spectacular care at my local 24-hour pet emergency clinic, they both received immediate treatment and healed nicely."

~ Gene T., Ventura, CA

NORTH DAKOTA

Bismarck - *Burleigh County*
Bismarck Animal Clinic & Hospital
1414 East Calgary Avenue
Bismarck, ND 58503
Phone: (701) 222-8255
Fax: --
Website: --
Hours: Call - 24 hours.

Fargo - *Cass County*
Red River Animal Emergency Clinic
1401 Oak Manor Avenue
Fargo, ND 58103
Phone: (701) 478-9299
Fax: --
Website: --
Hours: Mon - Thurs (5pm-8am);
Weekends from Fri (5pm) -
Mon (8am); Holidays

Breeze

Grand Forks Area -
Grand Forks County
The following 3 veterinary clinics are
open on a rotational basis. Please call
first to find out which one is open at
the time of your call.

1) Kindness Animal Hospital
4400 32nd Avenue South
Grand Forks, ND 58201
Phone: (701) 772-7289
Fax: --
Website: --
Hours: Rotational with
Petcetera and Peterson

2) Petcetera Animal Clinic
1150 40th Avenue South
Grand Forks, ND 58201
Phone: (701) 775-0549
Toll Free: (800) 434-PETC
(outside Grand Forks area)
Fax: --
Website: www.petcgfk.com
Hours: Rotational with
Kindness and Peterson

3) Peterson Veterinary Clinic
1525 Central Avenue Northwest
East Grand Forks, MN 56721
Phone: (218) 773-2401
Fax: --
Website: --
Hours: Rotational with
Kindness and Petcetera

OHIO

Akron - *Summit County*
Akron Veterinary Referral &
   Emergency Center
1321 Centerview Circle
Akron, OH 44321
Phone: (330) 665-4996
Fax: (330) 665-5972
Website: www.akronvet.com
Hours: 24 hours a day; 7 days a week;
      365 days a year
Note: Daytime practice also at
      this location.

Bedford - *Cuyahoga County*
Veterinary Referral Clinic and
   Emergency Center
5035 Richmond Road
Bedford, OH 44146
Phone: (216) 831-6789
Fax: --
Website: --
Hours: Call for current
      emergency hours.

Bedford Heights - *Cuyahoga County*
Dr. Hart's Emergency Pet Clinic
25780 Miles Road - Suite H
Bedford Heights, OH 44146
Phone: (216) 464-2298
Fax: --
Website: www.drhartvetclinics.com
Hours: Mon, Tues, Thurs (6pm-
      8:30am); Wed (all day);
      Fri (6pm) to Mon (8:30am);
      Holidays

Sophie

Cincinnati - *Hamilton County*
Cincinnati Animal Referral &
   Emergency Care (CARE)
6995 East Kemper Road
Cincinnati, OH 45249
Phone: (513) 530-0911
Fax: (513) 530-0811
Website: www.carecentervets.com
Hours: 24 hours a day;
      7 days a week;
      365 days a year

Emergency Veterinary Clinic of
   Cincinnati
4779 Red Bank Road
Cincinnati, OH 45227
Phone: (513) 561-0069
Fax: --
Website: --
Hours: 24 hours a day;
      7 days a week;
      365 days a year

Grady Veterinary Hospital
9255 Winton Road
Cincinnati, OH 45231
Phone: (513) 931-8675
Fax: (513) 931-4109
Website: www.gradyvet.com
Hours: 24 hours a day;
      7 days a week;
      365 days a year

Cleveland - *Cuyahoga County*
Animal Emergency Clinic
5320 West 140th Street
Cleveland, OH 44142
Phone: (216) 362-6000
Fax: --
Website: --
Hours: Mon - Fri (6pm-8am);
      Weekends from Sat (noon) -
      Mon (8am); Holidays

COLUMBUS - *Franklin County*
Ohio State University
College of Veterinary Medicine
1900 Coffey Road
Columbus, OH 43210
Phone: (614) 292-3551 Small Animal
(Companion Animal Care)
Phone: (614) 292-6661 Large Animal
(Farm Animal and Equine Care)
Website: www.vet.ohio-state.edu
Hours: Emergency Service - Call.

Columbus - *Franklin County*
Animal Medical &
Emergency Hospital
2527 West Dublin-Granville Road
Columbus, OH 43235
Phone: (614) 889-2556
Fax: --
Website: www.drdonn.com
Hours: 24 hours a day
Note: Please call for appointment.

Dayton - *Montgomery County*
Dayton Emergency Veterinary Clinic
2714 Springboro Road West
Dayton, OH 45439
Phone: (937) 293-2714
Fax: --
Website: --
Hours: Weeknights (6pm-7am);
Weekends & Major Holidays -
24 hours

Girard - *Trumbull County*
After Hours Animal Emergency Clinic
2680 West Liberty Street
Girard, OH 44420
Phone: (330) 530-8387
Fax: (330) 545-9051
Website: --
Hours: Mon - Fri (6pm-8am);
Weekends from Sat (noon) -
Mon (8am); Holidays

Lorain - *Lorain County*
Lorain County Animal
Emergency Hospital Center
1909 North Ridge Road
Lorain, OH 44055
Phone: (440) 240-1400
Fax: --
Website: --
Hours: Mon - Fri (6pm-8am);
Weekends from Sat (noon) -
Mon (8am); Holidays

(Ohio continues)

Ming

OHIO (continued)

Madisonville - *Hamilton County*
Emergency Veterinary Clinic
    of Cincinnati
4779 Red Bank Road
Madisonville, OH 45243
Phone: (513) 561-0069
Fax: --
Website: --
Hours: 24 hours a day;
        7 days a week;
        365 days a year

Mentor - *Lake County*
Animal Emergency Clinics
8250 Tyler Boulevard
Mentor, OH 44060
Phone: (440) 255-0770
Fax: --
Website: --
Hours: Mon - Fri (6pm-8am);
        Weekends from Sat (noon) -
        Mon (8am)

Shasta

Perrysburg - *Wood County*
Animal Weekend Emergency Clinic
399 West Boundary Street
Perrysburg, OH 43551
Phone: (419) 874-3148
Fax: (419) 874-3149
Website: --
Hours: Night & Weekend
        emergencies must call
        before proceeding
Note: Daytime practice also at
        this location.

Toledo - *Lucas County*
Animal Emergency and
    Critical Care Center of Toledo, Inc.
2785 West Central Avenue
Toledo, OH 43606
Phone: (419) 473-0328
Fax: (419) 473-0115
Website: www.animalertoledo.com
Hours: Weeknights (6pm-8am);
        Weekends & Major Holidays -
        24 hours

Worthington - *Franklin County*
MedVet
300 East Wilson Bridge Road
Worthington, OH 43085
Phone: (614) 846-5800
Toll Free: (800) 891-9010
Fax: (614) 846-5803
Website: www.medvet-cves.com
Hours: 24 hours a day;
        7 days a week;
        365 days a year

OKLAHOMA

Oklahoma City - *Cleveland County*
After Hours Emergency Pet Hospital
9225 South Interstate 35 Street
Oklahoma City, OK 73160
Phone: (405) 703-1741
Fax: --
Website: --
Hours: Mon - Fri (6pm-8am);
Weekends from Sat (noon) -
Mon (8am); Holidays

Animal Emergency Center
931 West I 240 Service Road (also
known as 931 SW 74th Street)
Oklahoma City, OK 73139
Phone: (405) 631-7828
Fax: (405) 631-7824
Website: --
Hours: Mon - Fri (6pm-8am);
Weekends from Sat (noon) -
Mon (8am); Holidays

Neel Veterinary Hospital
2700 North MacArthur Boulevard
Oklahoma City, OK 73127
Phone: (405) 947-8387
Fax: --
Website: www.neelvet.com
Hours: 24 hours a day;
7 days a week;
365 days a year

Veterinary Emergency and
Critical Care Hospital
1800 West Memorial Road
Oklahoma City, OK 73134
Phone 1: (405) 749-6993
Phone 2: (405) 749-6989
Fax: --
Website: --
Hours: 24 hours a day;
7 days a week;
365 days a year

STILLWATER - *Payne County*
Oklahoma State University
Center for Veterinary Health Sciences
Stillwater, OK 74708
Phone: (405) 744-7000
Option 1: Small Animal Clinic
Option 2: Large Animal Clinic
Option 3: Other areas of Hospital
Website: www.cvm.okstate.edu
Hours: Emergency services are
available 24 hours a day;
7 days a week.

Tulsa - *Tulsa County*
Animal Emergency Center, Inc.
7220 East 41st Street
Tulsa, OK 74145
Phone: (918) 665-0508
Fax: --
Website: www.aec-tulsa.com
Hours: Mon - Fri (6pm-8am);
Weekends from Sat (noon) -
Mon (8am); Holidays

Elvis

OREGON

Bend - *Deschutes County*
Animal Emergency Center of
    Central Oregon
1245 South East 3rd Street - Suite C3
Bend, OR 97702
Phone: (541) 385-9110
Fax: --
Website: www.bendaec.com
Hours: Mon - Fri (5pm-8am);
        Sat & Sun & Holidays - 24 hrs

Clackamas - *Clackamas County*
Northwest Veterinary Specialists
16756 South East 82nd Drive
Clackamas, OR 97015
Phone: (503) 656-3999
Fax: --
Website:
    www.northwestvetspecialists.com
Hours: Mon - Fri (6pm-8am);
        Sat & Sun & Holidays - 24 hrs

Stella

CORVALLIS - *Benton County*
Oregon State University
South West 30th Street
Corvallis, OR 97331
Phone: (541) 737-4812 or 4813
    Small Animal Hospital
Phone: (541) 737-2858
    Large Animal Hospital
Website: http://oregonstate.edu
Note: As of this writing, the Small
        Animal Clinic does not offer
        emergency services. Referrals
        are taken. Please call.

Corvallis - *Benton County*
Animal Emergency &
    Critical Care Center (located at
    Willamette Veterinary Clinic)
650 South West 3rd Street
Corvallis, OR 97333
Phone: (541) 753-2223 Main Number
Phone: (541) 753-5750 Emergency
Fax: --
Website: www.wvcvets.com
Hours: 24 hours a day;
        7 days a week;
        365 days a year

Medford - *Jackson County*
Southern Oregon Veterinary
    Specialty Center
3265 Biddle Road
Medford, OR 97504
Phone: (541) 282-7711
Fax: --
Website: www.sousc.com
Hours: 24 hours a day

Portland - *Multnomah County*
Dove Lewis Emergency
    Animal Hospital-Southeast
10564 South East Washington Street
Portland, OR 97215
Phone: (503) 262-7194
Fax: (503) 262-7198
Website: www.dovelewis.org
Hours: Mon - Thurs (6pm-8am);
        Weekends from Fri (6pm) -
        Mon (8am); Holidays

Dove Lewis Emergency Animal
    Hospital-Northwest
1945 North West Pettygrove Street
Portland, OR 97209
Phone: (503) 228-7281
Fax: (503) 228-0464
Website: www.dovelewis.org
Hours: 24 hours a day

VCA Southeast Portland
  Animal Hospital
13830 South East Stark Street
Portland, OR 97233
Phone: (503) 255-8139
Fax: (503) 257-2081
Website: www.vcasoutheast.com
Hours: 24 hours a day;
      7 days a week;
      365 days a year

Salem - *Marion County*
Salem Veterinary Emergency Clinic
3215 Market Street Northeast
Salem, OR 97301
Phone: (503) 588-8082
Fax: --
Website: --
Hours: Mon - Fri (5pm-8am);
      Sat & Sun & Holidays - 24 hrs

Springfield - *Lane County*
Eugene-Springfield Emergency
  Veterinary Hospital
103 Q Street
Springfield, OR 97477
Phone: (541) 746-0112
Fax: --
Website: --
Hours: 24 hours a day;
      7 days a week;
      365 days a year

Tualatin - *Washington County*
Emergency Veterinary Clinic
19314 South West Mohave Court
Tualatin, OR 97062
Phone: (503) 691-7922
Fax: --
Website: --
Hours: Mon - Thurs (6pm-8am);
      Weekends from Fri (6pm) -
      Mon (8am)

Alfie chewing on mom, Roxanne

PENNSYLVANNIA

Castle Shannon - *Allegheny County*
VCA Castle Shannon
3610 Library Road
Castle Shannon, PA 15234
Phone: (412) 885-2500
Fax: (412) 885-8901
Website: --
Hours: 24 hours

Erie - *Erie County*
Pet Emergency Center
429 West 38th Street
Erie, PA 16508
Phone: (814) 866-5920
Fax: --
Website: --
Hours: Mon - Fri (8pm-8am);
    Weekends from Sat (2pm) -
    Mon (8am)

Lancaster - *Lancaster County*
Pet Emergency Treatment Services
930 North Queen Street
Lancaster, PA 17603
Phone: (717) 295-7387
Fax: (717) 295-1948
Website:
    www.lancasterpetemergency.com
Hours: Mon - Thurs (6pm-8am);
    Weekends from Fri (6pm) -
    Mon (8am); Holidays

Travis

Langhorne - *Bucks County*
Center for Animal Referral and
    Emergency Service (formerly The
    Animal Emergency and Critical Care)
2010 Cabot Boulevard West - Suite D
Langhorne, PA 19047
Phone: (215) 750-2774
Fax: (215) 750-3623
Website: www.vetcares.com
Hours: 24 hours a day;
    7 days a week;
    365 days a year

Veterinary Specialty and
    Emergency Center
1900 West Old Lincoln Highway
Langhorne, PA 19047
Phone: (215) 750-7884
Fax: (215) 752-3156
Website: www.vsecvet.com
Hours: 24 hours a day;
    Weekends & Holidays

Lansdale - *Montgomery County*
Gwynedd Veterinary Hospital and
    Emergency Service
1615 West Point Pike
Lansdale, PA 19446
Phone: (215) 699-9294
Fax: (215) 699-7754
Website:
    www.gwyneddvethospital.com
Hours: 24 hours a day; 365 days a year

Malvern - *Chester County*
Veterinary Referral Center &
    Emergency Service
340 Lancaster Pike
Malvern, PA 19355
Phone: (610) 647-2950
Fax: (610) 296-3835
Website: www.vetreferral.com
Hours: 24 hours a day;
    7 days a week;
    365 days year

Mechanicsburg - *Cumberland County*
Animal Emergency Medical Center
11 Willow Mill Park Road
Mechanicsburg, PA 17050
Phone: (717) 796-2334
Fax: --
Website: --
Hours: Mon - Fri (8pm-7am);
Weekends from Sat (noon) -
Mon (7am)

Tasha

Monroeville - *Montgomery County*
Allegheny Veterinary Emergency
Trauma & Specialty
4224 Northern Pike
Monroeville, PA 15146
Phone: (412) 373-4200
Fax: (412) 373-4250
Website: www.avets.us
Hours: 24 hours; 7 days; 365 days

Norristown - *Montgomery County*
Metropolitan Emergency Service
2626 Van Buren Avenue
Norristown, PA 19403
Phone: (610) 666-0914 Emergency
Phone: (610) 666-1050
Fax: (610) 666-1199
Website: www.metro-vet.com
Hours: 24 hours a day;
7 days a week;
365 days year

PHILADELPHIA -
Philadelphia County
University of Pennsylvania
Matthew J. Ryan Veterinary Hospital
3800 Spruce Street
Philadelphia, PA 19104
Phone: (215) 746-V911 (215-746-8911)
Emergency 24 hours a day
Phone: (215) 746-VETS (215-746-8387)
Appointments
Website: www.vet.upenn.edu
Hours: Emergency services are
available 24 hours a day;
7 days a week.

Pittsburgh - *Allegheny County*
Metropolitan Veterinary Center
5309 Campbells Run Road
Pittsburgh, PA 15226
Phone: (412) 788-6400
Fax: (412) 749-1241
Website: --
Hours: 24 hours a day

Metropolitan Veterinary Center
560 McNeilly Road
Pittsburgh, PA 15226
Phone: (412) 344-6888
Fax: (412) 344-5459
Website: --
Hours: 24 hours a day

Pittston - *Luzerne County*
Animal Emergency Clinic of
Wyoming Valley
755 Township Boulevard
Pittston, PA 18640
Phone: (570) 655-3600
Fax: (570) 655-0960
Website: www.aecwv.com
Hours: 24 hours a day; 7 days a week

(Pennsylvania continues)

PENNSYLVANIA (continued)

Plum - *Allegheny County*
Allegheny Veterinary Emergency
1810 Golden Mile Highway
Plum, PA 15239
Phone: (724) 325-1881
Fax: --
Website: --
Hours: 24 hours a day

Plymouth Meeting -
Montgomery County
Pennsylvania Veterinary Specialty &
Emergency Associates (located at
Hickory Veterinary Hospital)
2303 Hickory Road
Plymouth Meeting, PA 19462
Phone: (610) 828-3054
Fax: (610) 828-0811
Website: www.hickoryvet.com
Hours: staffed 24 hours a day

Quakertown - *Bucks County*
Quakertown Veterinary Clinic
2250 North Old Bethlehem Pike
Quakertown, PA 18951
Phone: (215) 536-6245 Small Animal
Phone: (215) 536-2726 Large Animal
Fax: --
Website:
www.quakertownvetclinic.com
Hours: 24 hours a day;
7 days a week;
365 days a year

Saylorsburg - *Monroe County*
Creature Comforts Veterinary Service
Old Route 115
Saylorsburg, PA 18353
Phone: (570) 992-0400
Fax: (570) 992-4713
Website: www.creaturecomfortsvet.net
Hours: 24 hours a day;
7 days a week

Scotrun - *Monroe County*
Pocono Veterinary Emergency &
Critical Care Center
19 Scotrun Drive
Scotrun, PA 18355
Phone: (570) 620-1800
Fax: --
Website: --
Hours: Weeknights (7pm-8am);
Weekends & Major Holidays -
24 hours

Shaler - *Allegheny County*
Veterinary Emergency Clinic
882 Butler Street (Route 8)
Shaler, PA 15223
Phone: (412) 492-9855
Fax: --
Website: --
Hours: Mon - Fri (8pm-8am);
Sat & Sun & Holidays - 24 hrs

Shillington - *Berks County*
Berks Animal Emergency Center
(located at VCA Detwiler
Animal Hospital)
22 North Kenhorst Boulevard
Shillington, PA 19607
Phone: (610) 775-7535
Fax: --
Website: --
Hours: Weekends from Sat (noon) -
Mon (7:30am); Holidays;
Call for other hours.
Note: Daytime practice also at
this location.

Warrington - *Bucks County*
Bucks County Veterinary Emergency
   Trauma Services (V.E.T.S.)
978 Easton Road
Warrington, PA 18976
Phone: (215) 918-2200
Fax: --
Website: --
Hours: Mon - Thurs (6pm-8am);
      Weekends from Fri (6pm) -
      Mon (8am); Holidays

Watsontown -
Northumberland County
Animal Emergency Center
395 Susquehanna Trail
Watsontown, PA 17777
Phone: (570) 742-7400
Fax: --
Website: --
Hours: Mon - Fri (7pm-7am);
      Weekends from Sat (noon) -
      Mon (7am)

West Chester - *Chester County*
West Chester Animal
   Emergency Center (located at West
   Chester Veterinary Medical Center)
1141 West Chester Pike
West Chester, PA 19382
Phone: (610) 696-4110 Emergency
Phone: (610) 696-8712 Office
Fax: (610) 696-5948
Website:
   www.westchestervetmedclinic.com
Hours: Mon, Tues, Thurs (8pm-8am);
      Wed, Fri (6pm-8am);
      Sat (1pm) - Mon (8am);
      Holidays 24 hours
Note: Daytime practice also at
      this location.

Wexford - *Allegheny County*
Bradford Hills Emergency Clinic
13055 Perry Highway
Wexford, PA 15090
Phone: (724) 935-5827
Fax: --
Website: --
Hours: 24 hours a day; 7 days a week;
      365 days a year

Whitehall - *Lehigh County*
Valley Central Emergency
   Veterinary Hospital
210 Fullerton Avenue
Whitehall, PA 18052
Phone: (610) 435-5588
Fax: (610) 435-2690
Website: --
Hours: Mon - Thurs (8pm-8am);
      Weekends from Fri (5pm) -
      Mon (8am); Holidays

York - *York County*
Animal Emergency Clinic
3256 North Susquehanna Trail
York, PA 17402
Phone: (717) 767-5355
Fax: --
Website: --
Hours: Mon - Thurs (8pm-8am);
      Weekends from Fri (8pm) to
      Mon (8am)

Marvin

RHODE ISLAND

East Greenwich - *Kent County*
Ocean State Veterinary Specialists
1480 South County Trail
East Greenwich, RI 02818
Phone: (401) 886-6787
Fax: (401) 886-8998
Website: www.osvs.net
Hours: 24 hours a day;
　　　　7 days a week

Warwick - *Kent County*
Emergency Veterinary Services of
　Rhode Island
205 Hallene Road
Warwick, RI 02886
Phone: (401) 732-1811
Fax: --
Website: --
Hours: Mon - Thurs (5pm-9am);
　　　　Weekends from Fri (5pm) -
　　　　Mon (9am)

Monroe taking Grandpa and Emily for a walk

SOUTH CAROLINA

Columbia - *Richland County*
South Carolina Veterinary
　　Emergency Care
132 Stonemark Lane
Columbia, SC 29210
Phone: (803) 798-3837
Fax: (803) 561-9874
Website: www.scvec.com
Hours: Mon - Thurs (6pm-8am);
　　　　Weekends from Fri (6pm) -
　　　　Mon (8am); Holidays

Elgin - *Kershaw County*
Palmetto Regional Emergency
　　Hospital for Animals
921 Spears Creek Court
Elgin, SC 29045
Phone: (803) 865-1418
Fax: (803) 865-4018
Website: www.prehavet.com
Hours: 24 hours a day
Note: 　Pet emergency transportation
　　　　may be available.

Greenville - *Greenville County*
Animal Emergency Clinic
393 Woods Lake Road
Greenville, SC 29607
Phone: (864) 232-1878 Clinic
Phone: (864) 234-4701 Office
Fax: (864) 271-9378
Website: www.aecgreenville.com
Hours: Mon - Fri (6pm-8am);
　　　　Weekends from Sat (noon) -
　　　　Mon (8am); Holidays

Gil

Mount Pleasant - *Charleston County*
Greater Charleston Emergency
　　Veterinary Hospital
930 Pine Hollow Road
Mount Pleasant, SC 29464
Phone: (843) 216-7554
Fax: (843) 573-4906
Website: www.gcevc.com
Hours: Mon - Thurs (6pm-8am);
　　　　Weekends from Fri (6pm) -
　　　　Mon (8am); Holidays

Cookie

Myrtle Beach - *Horry County*
Animal Emergency Hospital of
　　the Strand
303 Highway 15 - Suite 1
Myrtle Beach, SC 29577
Phone: (843) 445-9797
Fax: --
Website: --
Hours: Mon - Fri (6pm-8am);
　　　　Weekends from Sat (1pm) -
　　　　Mon (8am); Holidays

(South Carolina continues)

SOUTH CAROLINA (continued)

North Charleston -
Charleston County
Greater Charleston Emergency
  Veterinary Clinic
3163 West Montague Avenue
North Charleston, SC 29418
Phone: (843) 744-3372
Fax: --
Website: www.gcevc.com
Hours: Mon - Thurs (6pm-8am);
    Weekends from Fri (6pm) -
    Mon (8am); Holidays

Spartanburg - *Spartanburg County*
Veterinary Emergency Clinic
1291 Asheville Highway
Spartanburg, SC 29303
Phone: (864) 591-1923
Fax: --
Website: --
Hours: Mon - Fri (6pm-8am);
    Weekends from Sat (noon) -
    Mon (8am); Holidays

SOUTH DAKOTA

Rapid City - *Pennington County*
Dakota Hills Veterinary Clinic
1571 East Highway 44
Rapid City, SD 57703
Phone: (605) 342-7498
Fax: (605) 342-9168
Website: --
Hours: Veterinarians/technicians on
staff 24 hours a day

Emergency Veterinary Hospital
(located at Animal Clinic)
1655 Valley Drive
Rapid City, SD 57703
Phone: (605) 721-0789 Emergency
Phone: (605) 342-1368 Main Number
Toll free: (888) 384-7743
Fax: (605) 721-0763
Website: --
Hours: 24 hours a day;
7 days a week;
365 days a year

Sioux Falls - *Minnehaha County*
Veterinary Emergency Hospital
3508 South Minnesota Avenue -
Suite 104
Sioux Falls, SD 57104
Phone: (605) 977-6200
Fax: (605) 335-4339
Website:
www.myvetonline.com/website/vetemergency
Hours: Mon - Fri (6pm-8am);
Weekends from Sat (noon) -
Mon (8am)

Watertown - *Codington County*
Howard Veterinary Clinic
1400 North Highway 20
Watertown, SD 57201-7562
Phone: (605) 882-4188
Fax: (605) 882-4746
Website: --
Hours: 24 hours a day

Harry

TENNESSEE

Alcoa - *Blount County*
Midland Pet Emergency Center
235 South Calderwood Road
Alcoa, TN 37701
Phone: (865) 982-1007
Fax: --
Website: --
Hours: Mon - Fri (6pm-7am);
       Weekends from Sat (1pm) -
       Mon (7am); Holidays

Blountville - *Sullivan County*
Airport Pet Emergency Clinic
2436 Highway 75
Blountville, TN 37617
Phone: (423) 279-0574
Fax: (423) 279-0858
Website: --
Hours: Mon - Thurs (6pm-8am);
       Weekends from Fri (6pm) -
       Mon (8am)

Brentwood - *Williamson County*
Pet Emergency Treatment
   Service (P.E.T.S.) (located at
   Affiliated Veterinary Specialists)
1668 Mallory Lane
Brentwood, TN 37027
Phone: (615) 333-1212
Fax: (615) 661-9883
Website: www.avs-pets.com
Hours: Mon - Fri (6:30pm-7am);
       Weekends from Sat (noon) -
       Mon (7am); Holidays

Charleston - *Bradley County*
Bradley Mc Minn Pet Emergency
9017 Hiwassee Street NW
Charleston, TN 37310
Phone: (423) 336-2822
Fax: --
Website: --
Hours: Mon - Fri (6pm-8am);
       Sat & Sun & Holidays - 24 hrs

Chattanooga - *Hamilton County*
River Vet Emergency Animal Clinic
2612 Amnicola Highway
Chattanooga, TN 37406
Phone: (423) 698-4612
Fax: --
Website: www.rivervetemergency.com
Hours: Mon - Fri (6:30pm-6:30am);
       Weekends from Sat (12:30pm)
       to Mon (6:30am);
       Holidays 24 hours

Columbia - *Maury County*
Animal Emergency of
   Maury County, LLC
1900 Shady Brook Street - Suite B
Columbia, TN 38401
Phone: (931) 380-1929
Fax: --
Website: --
Hours: Mon - Fri (6pm-7am);
       Weekends from Sat (noon) -
       Mon (7am)

Charlie

Cordova - *Shelby County*
Pet Med Veterinary Emergency
830 North Germantown Parkway -
   Suite 105
Cordova, TN 38018
Phone: (901) 624-9002
Fax: --
Website: --
Hours: Mon - Fri (6pm-8am);
        Sat & Sun & Holidays - 24 hrs
Note: Daytime practice also at
        this location.

Salem

Goodlettsville - *Davidson County*
Rivergate Pet Emergency Clinic
910 Meadow Lark Lane
Goodlettsville, TN 37072
Phone: (615) 859-3778
Fax: --
Website: --
Hours: Mon - Fri (7pm-7am);
        Weekends from Sat (5pm) -
        Mon (7am); Holidays

Jackson - *Madison County*
Jackson Pet Emergency Clinic
Towering Oaks Office Complex
2815 North Highland Avenue
Jackson, TN 38305
Phone: (731) 660-4343
Fax: --
Website: --
Hours: Mon - Thurs (6pm-7am);
        Weekends from Fri (6pm) -
        Mon (7am); Holidays

KNOXVILLE - *Knox County*
University of Tennessee
College of Veterinary Medicine
Small Animal Clinical Services (SACS)
Veterinary Teaching Hospital
2407 River Drive
Knoxville, TN 37996
Phone: (865) 974-8387
        Small Animal Clinic
Phone: (865) 974-5701
        Large Animal Clinic
Fax: --
Website: www.vet.utk.edu
Hours: Emergency services are
        available 24 hours a day;
        7 days a week.

Knoxville - *Knox County*
After Hours Pet Emergency Clinic
   (located at Veterinary Surgical
   Services)
215 Center Park Drive
Knoxville, TN 37922
Phone: (865) 966-3888 Emergency
Phone: (865) 966-3920 Main
Fax: --
Website:
   www.veterinarysurgicalservices.com
Hours: 24 hours a day

Knoxville Pet Emergency Clinic
1819 Ailor Avenue
Knoxville, TN 37921
Phone: (865) 637-0114
Fax: --
Website: --
Hours: Mon - Thurs (7pm-7am);
        Weekends from Fri (7pm) -
        Mon (7am); Holidays

(Tennessee continues)

TENNESSEE (continued)

Memphis - *Shelby County*
Animal Emergency Center, PC
3767 Summer Avenue
Memphis, TN 38122
Phone: (901) 323-4563
Fax: --
Website:
www.animalemergencycentermemphis.com
Hours: Mon -Thurs (6pm-8am);
       Weekends from Fri (6pm) -
       Mon (8am); Holidays

Murfreesboro - *Rutherford County*
Animal Medical Center
234 River Rock Boulevard
Murfreesboro, TN 37128
Phone: (615) 867-7575
Fax: --
Website: --
Hours: 24 hours a day;
       7 days a week;
       365 days a year

Nashville - *Davidson County*
Pet Emergency Clinic
2000 12th Avenue South
Nashville, TN 37204
Phone: (615) 383-2600
Fax: --
Website: --
Hours: Mon - Fri (7pm-7am);
       Weekends from Sat (5pm) -
       Mon (7am); Holidays

Talbott - Hamblen County
Five Rivers Pet Emergency Clinic
6057 West Andrew Johnson Highway -
   Suite 1
Nashville, TN 37204
Phone: (423) 581-9492
Fax: (423) 586-9786
Website: --
Hours: Mon - Fri (6pm-7am);
       Weekends from Sat (noon) -
       Mon (7am); Holidays

Pearl (aka "Pearly")

TEXAS

Abilene - *Taylor County*
Emergency Veterinary Clinic (located
    at Ridgemont Animal Clinic)
3981 Ridgemont Drive
Abilene, TX 79606
Phone: (325) 691-1504 Emergency
Phone: (325) 692-8412 Main
Fax: --
Website: www.ridgemontanimal.com
Hours: 24 hours a day; 7 days a week
Note: Regular appointments
         also available.

Arlington - *Tarrant County*
I-20 Animal Medical Center
5820 West I-20
Arlington, TX 76017
Phone: (817) 478-9238
Fax: --
Website: www.i20animaler.com
Hours: 24 hours a day;
        7 days a week;
        365 days a year

Austin - *Travis County*
Emergency Animal Hospital (North)
12034 Research Boulevard - Suite 8
Austin, TX 78759
Phone: (512) 331-6121
Fax: (512) 331-6591
Website: www.eahnwa.com
Hours: After hour Nights; Weekends;
        Holidays; 365 days a year

Emergency Animal Hospital (South)
4434 Frontier Trail
Austin, TX 78745
Phone: (512) 899-0955
Fax: (512) 892-7911
Website: www.eahnwa.com
Hours: After hour Nights; Weekends;
        Holidays; 365 days a year

Beaumont - *Jefferson County*
Southeast Texas Animal
    Emergency Clinic
3420 West Cardinal Drive
Beaumont, TX 77705
Phone: (409) 842-3239
Toll Free: (866) 374-7387
Fax: (409) 886-1066
Website: --
Hours: Mon - Thurs (6pm-7am);
        Weekends from Fri (6pm) -
        Mon (7am); Holidays

Benbrook - *Tarrant County*
Benbrook Animal Hospital
9009 Benbrook Boulevard
Benbrook, TX 76126
Phone: (817) 249-2744
Fax: --
Website: --
Hours: Nights; Weekends; Holidays
Note: Call for current hours.

Burleson - *Johnson County*
Burleson Animal Emergency Hospital
805 North East Alsbury Boulevard -
    Suite B
Burleson, TX 76028
Phone: (817) 447-9194
Fax: --
Website: www.burlesonanimaler.com
Hours: Mon - Thurs (6pm-8am);
        Weekends from Fri (6pm) -
        Mon (8am)

(Texas continues)

TEXAS (continued)

Carrollton - *Denton County*
North Texas Emergency Pet Clinic
1712 West Frankford Road - Suite 108
Carrollton, TX 75007
Phone: (972) 323-1310
Toll Free: (800) 362-8600
Fax: (972) 466-3721
Website: www.ntepc.com
Hours: Call for current
emergency hours.

Forrest

COLLEGE STATION -
Brazos County
Texas A & M University
Veterinary Medical Teaching Hospital
University College of
Veterinary Medicine
University Drive
College Station, TX 77840
Phone: (979) 845-2351 Main
Phone: (888) 778-5523
Veterinarian Referral
Fax: (979) 845-6978
Website: www.cvm.tamu.edu
Hours: Emergency services are
available 24 hours a day;
7 days a week.

Conroe - *Montgomery County*
Animal Emergency Clinic
920 West Dallas Street
Conroe, TX 77301
Phone 1: (936) 539-3800
Phone 2: (936) 441-4631
(alternate phone)
Fax: --
Website: --
Hours: Weeknights (6pm-8am);
Weekends from Sat (noon) -
Mon (8am)

Corpus Christi - *Nueces County*
Northwest Animal Emergency Center
(located at Nueces Veterinary Hospital)
11027 Leopard Street
Corpus Christi, TX 78410
Phone: (361) 242-3999 Emergency
Phone: (361) 242-3337 Main
Fax: --
Website: www.nuecesvethospital.com
Hours: 24 hours a day;
7 days a week;
365 days a year
Note: Daytime practice also at
this location.

Oso Creek Animal Hospital &
Emergency Center
7713 South Staples Street
Corpus Christi, TX 78413
Phone: (361) 994-1145
Fax: (361) 994-0178
Website: --
Hours: Call for current
emergency hours.

Dallas - *Dallas County*
Emergency Animal Clinic
12101 Greenville Avenue - Suite 118
Dallas, TX 75243
Phone: (972) 994-9110
Fax: --
Website:
www.emergencyanimalclinicdallas.com
Hours: Mon - Thurs (6pm-8am);
      Weekends from Fri (6pm) -
      Mon (8am); Holidays

Groucho

The E-Clinic Veterinary Emergency
3337 North Fitzhugh Avenue
Dallas, TX 75204
Phone: (214) 520-8388
Fax: (214) 780-0992
Website: www.eclinic.org
Hours: Mon - Thurs (6pm-8am);
      Weekends from Fri (6pm) -
      Mon (8am); Holidays 24 hours

Denton - *Denton County*
Denton County Animal
   Emergency Room
4145 South Interstate 35 East -
   Suite 101
Denton, TX 76210
Phone: (940) 271-1200
Toll Free: (800) 876-0060
Fax: (940) 271-1206
Website: www.dcaer.org
Hours: Mon - Thurs (5pm-8am);
      Weekends from Fri (5pm) -
      Mon (8am); Holidays

El Paso - *El Paso County*
Animal Emergency Center
1220 Airway Boulevard
El Paso, TX 79925
Phone: (915) 545-1148
Fax: --
Website: --
Hours: Mon - Thurs (5:30pm-8am);
      Weekends from Fri (5:30pm) -
      Mon (8am); Holidays

Euless - *Tarrant County*
Airport Freeway Animal
   Emergency Clinic
411 North Main Street
Euless, Texas 76039
Phone: (817) 571-2088
Fax: (817) 571-1871
Website: www.afaec.com
Hours: Mon - Fri (6pm-8am);
      Sat & Sun & Holidays - 24 hrs

Fort Worth - *Tarrant County*
Metro West Emergency
   Veterinary Center (located at
   Hulen Hills Animal Hospital)
3201 Hulen Street (at I-30)
Fort Worth, TX 76107
Phone: (817) 731-3734
Fax: (817) 731-4798
Website: www.metrowestvet.com
Hours: Mon - Fri (6pm-7:30am);
      Weekends from Sat (noon) -
      Mon (7:30am); Holidays
Note 1: Daytime practice also at
      this location.
Note 2: Center is looking to become
      a 24-hour facility.

(Texas continues)

TEXAS (continued)

Greenville - *Hunt County*
Emergency Veterinary Service
2809 Interstate Highway 30 East
Greenville, TX 75402
Phone: (903) 455-8588
Fax: --
Website: --
Hours: Nights & Holidays Only -
Call for current emergency
hours.

Patches

Houston - *Harris County*
Animal Emergency Center of
West Houston
4823 Highway 6 North
Houston, TX 77084
Phone: (832) 593-8387
Fax: (832) 593-8388
Website: www.aecwh.com
Hours: Weeknights (6pm-7:30am);
Weekends & Major Holidays -
24 hours

Animal Emergency Clinic
8921 Katy Freeway
Houston, TX 77024
Phone: (713) 932-9589
Fax: --
Website: --
Hours: Weeknights (6pm-7:30am);
Weekends & Holidays -
24 hours

Animal Emergency Clinic (located
at Cypresswood Veterinary
Surgery Center)
19311 State Highway 249
Houston, TX 77070
Phone: (281) 890-8875
Fax: (281) 890-7160
Website: www.aecsh249.com
Hours: Mon - Fri (6pm-8am);
Weekends from Fri (6pm) -
Mon (8am); Holidays
Note: Daytime practice also at
this location.

Animal Emergency Clinic
1111 West Loop South - Suite 200
Houston, TX 77027
Phone: (713) 693-1100
Fax: (713) 693-1101
Website:
www.animalemergencyhospital.com
Hours: Mon - Thurs (6pm-8am);
Weekends from Fri (6pm) -
Mon (8am); Holidays

VCA Animal Emergency
Clinic Southeast
10331 Gulf Freeway
Houston, TX 77034
Phone: (713) 941-8460
Fax: (713) 941-8523
Website: www.vcaemergencyse.com
Hours: Mon - Fri (6pm-8am);
Weekends from Sat (8am) -
Mon (8am)

Honey

Humble - *Harris County*
Animal Emergency Clinic North East
9617 Old 1960 Bypass Road
Humble, TX 77338
Phone: (281) 446-4900
Fax: --
Website: --
Hours: Weeknights (6pm-8am);
       Weekends & Holidays - 24 hrs

Irving - *Dallas County*
Metroplex Veterinary Centre
700 West Airport Freeway
Irving, TX 75062
Phone: (972) 438-7113
Fax: (972) 554-1894
Website: www.vcametroplex.com
Hours: 24 hours a day; 7 days a week

Killeen - *Bell County*
After Hours Veterinary Services
2501 South W.S. Young
Killeen, Texas 76542
Phone: (254) 628-5017
Fax: (254) 628-5491
Website: --
Hours: Mon - Fri (6pm-8am);
       Weekends from Sat (noon) -
       Mon (8am)

League City - *Galveston County*
VCA Animal Emergency Clinic SE-
   Calder Road
1100 Gulf Freeway South - Suite 104
League City, TX 77573
Phone: (281) 332-1678
Fax: (281) 332-7999
Website: www.vcacalderroad.com
Hours: Mon - Thurs (6pm-8am);
       Weekends from Fri (6pm) -
       Mon (8am)

Longview - *Gregg County*
East Texas Pet Emergency
812 Gilmer Road
Longview, TX 75604
Phone: (903) 759-8545
Fax: --
Website: --
Hours: Mon - Fri (6pm-7am);
       Weekends from Sat (1pm) -
       Mon (7am)

Lubbock - *Lubbock County*
Small Animal Emergency Clinic
5103 34th Street - Suite A
Lubbock, TX 79410
Phone: (806) 797-6483
Fax: --
Website: --
Hours: Mon - Fri (6pm-7am);
       Weekends from Sat (noon) -
       Mon (7am)

McKinney - *Collin County*
Emergency Animal Hospital
421 Oakwood Trail
McKinney, TX 75069
Phone: (972) 547-9900
Fax: --
Website: --
Hours: Nights; Weekends; Holidays

Mesquite - *Dallas County*
Lake Ray Hubbard Emergency
   Pet Care Center
4651 Belt Line
Mesquite, TX 75150
Phone: (972) 226-3377
Fax: --
Website: www.emergencypet.com
Hours: Mon - Thurs (6pm-7am);
       Weekends from Fri (6pm) -
       Mon (7am); Holidays

(Texas continues)

TEXAS (continued)

New Braunfels - *Comal County*
Emergency Pet Clinic
280 North Business 35
New Braunfels, TX 78130
Phone: (830) 609-2873
Fax: --
Website:
    www.emergencypetclinic.com
Hours: Call for new hours.

Odessa - *Ector County*
Permian Basin Emergency Clinic
13528 West Highway 80 E
Odessa, TX 79765
Phone: (432) 561-8301
Phone: (432) 520-4150
Fax: --
Website: --
Hours: After 7pm evenings; call for
    additional information.
Note: Daytime practice also at
    this location.

Mephisto and Van Dyke

Plano - *Collin County*
Emergency Animal Clinic of
    Collin County
10225 Custer Road
Plano, TX 75025
Phone: (214) 547-9900
Fax: --
Website:
    www.emergencyanimalclinic.net
Hours: Mon - Fri (6pm-8am);
    Weekends from Sat (noon) -
    Mon (8am); Holidays

Richardson - *Dallas County*
Emergency Animal Clinic
401 West President George Bush
    Highway
Richardson, TX 75080
Phone: (972) 479-9110
Fax: --
Website:
www.emergencyanimalclinicdallas.com
Hours: Mon - Thurs (6pm-8am);
    Weekends from Fri (6pm) -
    Mon (8am); Holidays

Round Rock - *Williamson County*
Emergency Animal Clinic
2000 North Mays Street - Suite 112
Round Rock, TX 78664
Phone: (512) 671-6252
Fax: (512) 733-8573
Website: www.aecctx.com
Hours: Mon - Fri (6pm-7am);
    Weekends from Sat (noon) -
    Mon (7am)

San Antonio - *Bexar County*
Angel Of Mercy Animal Critical Care
8734 Grissom Road
San Antonio, TX 78251
Phone: (210) 684-2105
Fax: (210) 256-0088
Website: --
Hours: Mon - Thurs (6pm-8am);
    Weekends from Fri (6pm) -
    Mon (8am); Holidays

Animal Emergency Room
4315 Fredericksburg Road - Suite 2
San Antonio, TX 78201
Phone: (210) 737-7380
Fax: --
Website: www.animaler.net
Hours: Weeknights (6pm-9am);
Weekends & Holidays - 24 hours

Emergency Pet Clinic -
  Broadway Location
8503 Broadway Street - Suite 105
San Antonio, TX 78217
Phone: (210) 822-2873
Fax: (210) 822-3036
Website: www.emergencypetclinic.com
Hours: 24 hours a day;
        7 days a week

Emergency Pet Center -
  Sonterra Location
503 East Sonterra Boulevard - Suite 103
San Antonio, TX 78258
Phone: (210) 404-2873
Fax: (210) 858-0133
Website: www.emergencypetclinic.com
Hours: After hour care;
        Call for details.

Emergency Pet Center -
  SE Military Location
3130 South East Military Drive -
  Suite 101
San Antonio, TX 78223
Phone: (210) 337-2873
Fax: --
Website: www.emergencypetclinic.com
Hours: After hour care;
        Call for details.

Southlake - *Tarrant County*
Animal Emergency Hospital of
  North Texas
2340 West Southlake Boulevard
Southlake, TX 76092
Phone: (817) 410-2273
Fax: --
Website: www.aehnt.com
Hours: Mon - Thurs (4pm-8am);
        Weekends from Fri (4pm) -
        Mon (8am); Holidays

Sylvie

Stafford - *Sherman County*
Sugar Land Veterinary Specialty and
  Emergency Center
12503 Exchange Drive
Stafford, TX 77477
Phone: (281) 491-7800
Fax: (281) 242-9750
Website: www.slvetspecialists.com
Hours: 24 hours a day;
        7 days a week;
        365 days a year
Note: New address 12/2007 will be
       1515 Lake Pointe Parkway
       in Sugar Land, TX. Phone
       numbers will not change.

Sugar Land - *Fort Bend County*
Veterinary Emergency Center
9920 Highway 90A
Sugar Land, TX 77478
Phone: (281) 340-8387
Fax: (281) 340-8388
Website: --
Hours: Mon - Fri (6pm-8am);
        Sat & Sun & Holidays - 24 hrs

Sugar Land Veterinary Specialty and
  Emergency Center
Note: This facility will move from
       Stafford to Sugar Land in
       December 2007. Refer to
       information above.

(Texas continues)

TEXAS (continued)

The Woodlands -
Montgomery County
Animal Emergency &
    Urgent Care Center
27870 I-45 North
The Woodlands, TX 77385
Phone: (281) 367-5444
Fax: (281) 367-5404
Website: www.aeucc.com
Hours: Mon - Fri (6pm-8am);
        Sat & Sun & Holidays - 24 hrs

Tyler - *Smith County*
Tyler Animal Emergency Clinic
3364 South Loop 323 SW
Tyler, TX 75701
Phone: (903) 534-0459
Fax: --
Website: --
Hours: Mon - Thurs (6pm-7:30am);
        Weekends from Fri (6pm) -
        Mon (7:30am)

Waco - *McLennan County*
Animal Emergency Clinic
3901 Jack Kultgen Freeway (I 35 South)
Waco, TX 76711
Phone: (254) 752-6100
Fax: (254) 235-9147
Website: www.aecwaco.com
Hours: Mon - Fri (6pm-7am);
        Weekends from Sat (noon) -
        Mon (7am)

Kirby

UTAH

Draper - *Salt Lake County*
Draper All Pet Emergency
12720 Pony Express Road
Draper, UT 84020
Phone: (801) 553-8899 Emergency
Phone: (801) 565-1263 Main
Fax: (801) 565-1287
Web: www.birdexoticpethospital.com
Hours: Open daily 'after hours' and
    all day Sunday.
Notes: (1) Daytime practice also at
      this location.
    (2) Emergency services
      available for dog, cat,
      and exotics.

Sundance

Orem - *Utah County*
Pet Med Center (located at
  Pet Medical Center of Utah Valley)
525 South State Street
Orem, UT 84058
Phone: (801) 225-5395
Fax: --
Website: --
Hours: After hour care; Call for
    details.
Note: Daytime practice also at
    this location.

Pet Urgent Care
428 West 800 North
Orem, UT 84057
Phone: (801) 765-1010
Fax: --
Website: --
Hours: Nights; Weekends;
    Holidays

Saint George - *Washington County*
Southwest Animal Emergency
435 North 1680 East - Suite 11
Saint George, UT 84790
Phone: (435) 673-3191
Fax: --
Website: --
Hours: Call for current
    emergency hours.

Salt Lake City - *Salt Lake County*
Salt Lake City Pet E.R. (located at
  Cottonwood Animal Hospital)
6360 South Highland Drive
Salt Lake City, UT 84121
Phone: (801) 278-3367
Fax: --
Website: --
Hours: 24 hours a day
Note: Daytime practice also at
    this location.

Sandy - *Salt Lake County*
Southeast Valley Animal Emergency
10572 South 700 E
Sandy, UT 84070
Phone: (801) 487-1325
Fax: --
Website: --
Hours: 24 hours a day
Note: Daytime practice also at
    this location.

(Utah continues)

UTAH (continued)

South Salt Lake - *Salt Lake County*
Central Emergency Animal
55 Miller Avenue
South Salt Lake, UT 84115
Phone: (801) 487-1325
Fax: --
Website:
www.centralvalleyvetgroup.com
Hours: Call for current
emergency hours.

Sunset - *Davis County*
Animal Emergency Center
2465 North Main Street - Suite 5
Sunset, UT 84015
Phone: (801) 776-8118
Fax: --
Website: --
Hours: Mon - Fri (6pm-8am);
Weekends from Sat (noon) -
Mon (8am); Holidays

Corsa

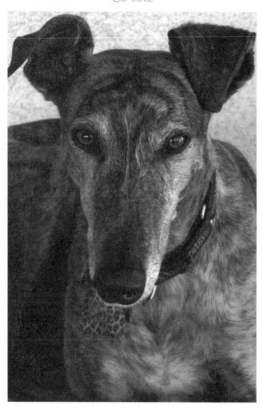

VERMONT

Williston - *Chittenden County*
Burlington Emergency Vet Service
200 Commerce Street
Williston, VT 05495
Phone: (802) 863-2387
Fax: --
Website: --
Hours: Mon - Fri (5pm-8am);
       Sat & Sun & Holidays - 24 hrs

Jenny

"*Last summer our two dogs, Emma and Nila, got into a porcupine on their morning walk. Emma took a BIG bite of porcupine. She had a terrible mess of quills far back into her throat and it was a lot of work to get them all out. The vets at the 'After Hours Veterinary Emergency Clinic' made us feel that we were in good hands and could relax, knowing that they would take care of things. Mark and I feel very fortunate that we have such a good veterinary emergency clinic here in Fairbanks.*"

~ Mark and Linda H., Fairbanks, AK

VIRGINIA

Alexandria - *Alexandria County*
Alexandria Animal Hospital and
    Veterinary Emergency Service
2660 Duke Street
Alexandria, VA 22314
Phone: (703) 751-2022 Day
Phone: (703) 823-3601 Night
Fax: (703) 370-8049
Website:
    www.alexandriaanimalhospital.com
Hours: 24 hours a day;
    7 days a week;
    365 days a year

BLACKSBURG -
Montgomery County
**Virginia Tech and
University of Maryland**
VA-MD Regional College of
    Veterinary Medicine
Virginia Tech, Duck Pond Drive
Blacksburg, VA 24061
Phone: (540) 231-4621 (Listen to
    menu options & respond
    accordingly.)
Website: www.vetmed.vt.edu
Note: Please call to discuss
    appointment options.

Lucky

Charlottesville -
    Charlottesville County
Veterinary Emergency Treatment
370 Greenbrier Drive - Suite A2
Charlottesville, VA 22901
Phone: (434) 973-3519
Fax: --
Website: www.emergency-vets.com
Hours: Mon - Fri (6pm-8am);
    Weekends from Sat (noon) -
    Mon (8am)

Fairfax - *Fairfax County*
Emergency Vet Clinic of Fair Oaks
4001 Legato Road
Fairfax, VA 22033
Phone: (703) 591-3304
Fax: (703) 591-6936
Website: www.evcfairoaks.com
Hours: 24 hours a day;
    7 days a week;
    365 days a year

SouthPaws
8500 Arlington Boulevard
Fairfax, VA 22031
Phone: (703) 752-9100
Fax: (703) 752-9200
Website: www.southpaws.com
Hours: 24 hours a day;
    7 days a week;
    365 days a year

Fredericksburg -
    Spotsylvania County
Animal Emergency Clinic of
    Fredericksburg
1210 Snowden Street
Fredericksburg, VA 22401
Phone: (540) 371-0554
Fax: --
Website: --
Hours: Mon - Fri (6pm-7am);
    Weekends from Sat (noon) -
    Mon (7am); Holidays

Fredericksburg Regional Veterinary
   Emergency Center
2301 Jefferson Davis Highway
Fredericksburg, VA 22401
Phone: (540) 372-3470
Fax: --
Website: --
Hours: Mon - Fri (6pm-8am);
      Weekends from Sat (noon) -
      Mon (8am); Holidays
Note: Looking to transition to
     24 hour facility.

Rusty

Leesburg - *Loudoun County*
Animal Emergency Hospital
2 Cardinal Park Drive - Suite 101B
Leesburg, VA. 20175
Phone: (703) 777-5755
Fax: (703) 777-9968
Website:
   www.animalemergencyhosp.com
Hours: 24 hours a day;
     7 days a week;
     365 days a year

Lynchburg - *Campbell County*
Animal Emergency and Critical Care
   of Lynchburg
3432 Odd Fellows Road
Lynchburg, VA 24501
Phone: (434) 846-1504
Fax: (434) 846-6407
Website: --
Hours: Mon - Fri (6pm-8am);
     Weekends from Sat (noon) -
     Mon (8am); Holidays

Manakin-Sabot - *Goochland County*
Veterinary Referral and Critical Care
1596 Hockett Road
Manakin-Sabot, VA 23103
Phone: (804) 784-8722
Fax: (804) 784-1960
Website: --
Hours: 24 hours a day

Manassas - *Prince William County*
Prince William Emergency
   Veterinary Clinic
8610 Centerville Road
Manassas, VA 20110
Phone: (703) 361-8287
Fax: (703) 361-8833
Website: www.princewilliamevc.com
Hours: Mon - Thurs (6pm-8am);
     Weekends from Fri (6pm) -
     Mon (8am); Holidays

Midlothian - *Chesterfield County*
Veterinary Emergency Center - South
12501 Hull Street
Midlothian, VA 23112
Phone: (804) 744-9800
Fax: (804) 744-4842
Website: www.animal-emergency.com
Hours: 24 hours a day; 7 days a week

Purcellville - *Loudoun County*
Blue Ridge Veterinary Associates
   Urgent Care
120 East Cornwell Lane
Purcellville, VA 20132
Phone: (540) 338-7387
Fax: (540) 338-6641
Website: www.blueridgevets.com
Hours: Weekends from Fri (7am) -
     Mon (9pm); Holidays;
     open late nights
Note: Looking to expand hours.

(Virginia continues)

VIRGINIA (continued)

Richmond - *Henrico County*
Veterinary Emergency Center -
  Carytown
3312 West Cary Street
Richmond, VA 23221
Phone: (804) 353-9000
Fax: (804) 353-9271
Website: www.animal-emergency.com
Hours: 24 hours a day; 7 days a week

Roanoke - *Roanoke County*
Emergency Veterinary Service
4902 Frontage Road NW
Roanoke, VA 24019
Phone: (540) 563-8575
Fax: --
Website: --
Hours: Mon - Fri (6pm-8am);
       Weekends from Sat (noon) -
       Mon (8am)

Fritz

Springfield - *Fairfax County*
The Regional Veterinary
  Referral Center
6651 Backlick Road
Springfield, VA 22150
Phone: (703) 451-8900
Fax: (703) 451-3343
Website: www.vetreferralcenter.com
Hours: 24 hours a day

SouthPaws Critical Care and
  Veterinary Referral Center
6136 Brandon Avenue
Springfield, VA 22150
Phone: (703) 569-0300
Fax: --
Website: --
Hours: 24 hours a day

Verona - *Augusta County*
Shenandoah Valley Regional
  Veterinary Emergency Services
  (SVRVES)
Verona Shopping Center
Route 11 (Lee Highway)
Verona, VA 24482
Phone: (540) 248-1051
Fax: --
Website: --
Hours: Mon - Fri (6pm-8am);
       Weekends from Sat (noon) -
       Mon (8am); Holidays

Vienna - *Fairfax County*
The Hope Center for
  Advanced Veterinary Medicine
416 Maple Avenue West
Vienna, VA 22180-4221
Phone: (703) 281-5121
Fax: (703) 281-0149
Website: www.hopecenter.com
Hours: 24 hours a day

Virginia Beach - *Virginia Beach County*
Beach Veterinary Emergency Center
1124 Lynnhaven Parkway
Virginia Beach, VA 23452
Phone: (757) 468-4900
Fax: --
Website: --
Hours: 24 hours a day; 7 days a week

Tidewater Veterinary Emergency &
   Critical Care Center
5425 Virginia Beach Boulevard
Virginia Beach, VA 23462
Phone: (757) 499-5463
Fax: (757) 499-3916
Website: --
Hours: 24 hours a day

Winchester - *Frederick County*
Valley Emergency Veterinary Clinic
164 Garber Lane
Winchester, VA 22602
Phone: (540) 662-7811
Fax: (540) 662-7870
Website: --
Hours: 24 hours a day; 7 days a week

Woodbridge - *Prince William County*
Woodbridge Animal Hospital
2703 Caton Hill Road
Woodbridge, VA 22192
Phone: (703) 897-5665
Fax: --
Website:
   www.woodbridgeanimalhospital.net
Hours: 24 hours a day;
       7 days a week;
       365 days a year

Yorktown - *York County*
Emergency Veterinary Clinic (located
   at Peninsula Veterinary Specialists)
1120 George Washington
   Memorial Highway (Route 17)
Yorktown, VA 23693
Phone: (757) 874-8115 Emergency
Phone: (757) 596-7100 Specialists
Fax: --
Website: www.peninsulavets.com
Hours: Mon - Fri (6pm-8am);
       Sat & Sun & Holidays - 24 hrs
Note: Daytime practice also at
       this location.

Blossom

WASHINGTON

(NOTE: For Washington, D.C., see District of Columbia)

Auburn - *King County*
After Hours Animal Emergency Clinic
718 Auburn Way North
Auburn, WA 98002
Phone: (253) 939-6272
Fax: --
Website: --
Hours: Mon - Fri (6pm-8am);
　　　　Weekends from Sat (noon) -
　　　　Mon (8am); Holidays

Bellevue - *King County*
After Hours Animal Emergency Clinic
　　(located at Aerowood Animal
　　Hospital)
2975 156th Avenue SE
Bellevue, WA 98007
Phone: (425) 746-6557
　　Regular Hospital Number
Phone: (425) 641-8414
　　After Hours Emergency
Fax: (425) 643-3609
Website:
www.aerowoodanimalhospital.vetsuite.com
Hours: 24 hours a day
Note: Daytime practice also at
　　　 this location.

Bellingham - *Whatcom County*
Animal Emergency Care
317 Telegraph Road
Bellingham, WA 98226
Phone: (360) 758-2200
Fax: --
Website: --
Hours: Mon - Fri (6pm-8am);
　　　　Weekends from Sat (noon) -
　　　　Mon (8am); Holidays

Bremerton - *Kitsap County*
Animal Emergency & Trauma Center
1526 Spruce Avenue
Bremerton, WA 98310
Phone: (360) 475-3077
Fax: --
Website: --
Hours: 24 hours a day;
　　　　7 days a week;
　　　　365 days a year

Burien - *King County*
VCA Five Corners Animal Hospital
15707 1st Avenue South
Burien, WA 98148
Phone: (206) 243-2982
Fax: (206) 248-0264
Website: www.vcafivecorners.com
Hours: 24 hours a day;
　　　　7 days a week;
　　　　365 days a year

Everett - *Snohomish County*
Animal Emergency Clinic of Everett
　　(located at Diamond Veterinary
　　Associates)
3625 Rucker Avenue
Everett, WA 98201
Phone: (425) 258-4466 Emergency
Phone: (425) 252-1106 Main
Fax: --
Website: www.diamondvet.com
Hours: Mon - Fri (6pm-8am);
　　　　Weekends from Sat (1pm) -
　　　　Mon (8am); Holidays

Issaquah - *King County*
Alpine Animal Hospital
888 North West Sammamish Road
Issaquah, WA 98027
Phone: (425) 392-8888
Fax: (425) 391-7439
Website: www.vcaalpinewa.com
Hours: 24 hours day; 7 days week

Kirkland - *King County*
Animal Emergency Services East
636 7th Avenue
Kirkland, WA 98033
Phone: (425) 827-8727
Fax: --
Website: --
Hours: Weekdays After 6pm;
     Weekends from Sat (noon) -
     Mon (8am); Holidays

Lacey - *Thurston County*
Olympia Pet Emergency
4242 Pacific Avenue
Lacey, WA 98503
Phone: (360) 455-5155
Fax: (360) 456-3583
Website: --
Hours: Mon - Thurs (6pm-7:30am);
     Weekends - 24 hours

Lynnwood - *Snohomish County*
Agape Pet Emergency Center
16418 7th Place West
Lynnwood, WA 98037
Phone: (425) 741-2688
Fax: (425) 742-1513
Website: --
Hours: Mon - Thurs (6pm-8am);
     Weekends from Fri (6pm) -
     Mon (8am)

VCA Veterinary Specialty
   Center of Seattle
20115 44th Avenue West
Lynnwood, WA 98036
Phone: (425) 697-6106
Fax: (425) 697-4746
Website: www.vcavsc.com
Hours: 24 hours a day;
     7 days a week;
     365 days a year

Pippi

Mount Vernon - *Skagit County*
Pet Emergency Center (PEC)
14434 Avon Allen Road
Mount Vernon, WA 98273
Phone: (360) 848-5911
Toll Free: (877) 848-5913 Emergency
Fax: --
Website: www.mypetemergency.com
Hours: 24 hours a day;
     7 days a week;
     365 days a year

Pasco - *Franklin County*
Pet Emergency Service
8913 Sandifur Parkway
Pasco, WA 99301
Phone: (509) 783-7391
Fax: --
Website: --
Hours: Mon - Fri (5pm-8am);
     Sat & Sun & Holidays - 24 hrs

(Washington continues)

WASHINGTON (continued)

Poulsbo - *Kitsap County*
Animal Emergency and
   Trauma Center
320 Lindvig Way
Poulsbo, WA 98370
Phone: (360) 697-7771
Fax: (360) 697-7934
Website: www.myaetc.com
Hours: 24 hours a day;
      7 days a week;
      365 days a year

VCA Central Kitsap Animal Hospital
10310 Central Valley Road NE
Poulsbo, WA 98370
Phone: (360) 692-6162
Fax: (360) 698-2456
Website: www.vcacentralkitsap.com
Hours: 24 hours a day;
      7 days a week;
      365 days a year

PULLMAN - *Whitman County*
Washington State University
Veterinary Teaching Hospital
NE Grimes Way
Pullman, WA 99164
Phone: (509) 335-0711
Website: www.vetmed.wsu.edu
Hours: Emergency services are
      available 24 hours a day,
      7 days a week, for small and
      large animals.

Seattle - *King County*
Animal Critical Care and
   Emergency Services (ACCES)
11536 Lake City Way NE
Seattle, WA 98125
Phone: (206) 364-1660
Fax: (206) 364-3667
Website: www.criticalcarevets.com
Hours: 24 hours a day;
      7 days a week;
      365 days a year

Emerald City Emergency Clinic
4102 Stone Way North
Seattle, WA 98103
Phone: (206) 634-9000
Fax: --
Website: --
Hours: Mon - Thurs (6pm-8am);
      Weekends from Fri (6pm) -
      Mon (8am); Holidays

VCA Five Corners
15707 1st Avenue
Seattle, WA 98148
Phone: (206) 243-2982
Fax: (206) 248-0264
Website: www.vcafivecorners.com
Hours: 24 hours a day; 7 days a week

Patti

Sedro Woolley - *Skagit County*
Pet Emergency Clinic
200 Murdock Street
Sedro Woolley, WA 98284
Phone: (360) 855-0513
Fax: --
Website: --
Hours: Call for current
      emergency hours.

Smokey

Snohomish - *Snohomish County*
Animal Emergency (located at
    Pilchuck Veterinary Hospital)
11308 92nd Street SE
Snohomish, WA 98290
Phone: (360) 568-9111
Toll Free: (800) 208-9192
Fax: (360) 568-1933
Website: www.pilchuckvet.com
Hours: Mon - Fri (6pm-8am);
        Weekends from Sat (8am) -
        Mon (8am)

Spokane - *Spokane County*
Pet Emergency Clinic
21 East Mission Avenue
Spokane, WA 99202
Phone: (509) 326-6670
Fax: --
Website: --
Hours: Weeknights (5pm-8am);
        Weekends & Major Holidays -
        24 hours

Sumner - *Pierce County*
Sumner Veterinary Hospital
16024 60th Street E
Sumner, WA 98390
Phone: (253) 863-2258
Fax: (253) 863-1488
Website: www.sumnervet.com
Note: Transitioning to 24 hour facility.

Tacoma - *Pierce County*
Puget Sound Veterinary Referral
    Center & The Animal Emergency
    Clinic
5608 South Durango Street
Tacoma, WA 98409
Phone: (253) 474-0791 Emergency
Fax: (253) 474-6057
Website: www.theaec.com
Hours: 24-hour, 7-day emergency and
        critical care center

Vancouver - *Clark County*
Clark County Emergency Vet Service
6818 North East Fourth Plain Blvd.
Vancouver, WA 98661
Phone: (360) 694-3007
Fax: --
Website: --
Hours: 24 hours a day;
        7 days a week;
        365 days a year

St Francis 24 Hr Animal Hospital
12010 Northeast 65th Street
Vancouver, WA 98682
Phone: (360) 253-5446
Fax: (360) 253-5446
Website: www.stfrancis24hr.com
Hours: 24 hours day

Yakima - *Yakima County*
Pet Emergency Service of Yakima
510 West Chestnut Avenue
Yakima, WA 98902
Phone: (509) 452-4138
Fax: --
Website: --
Hours: Weekends Only from
        Fri (5pm) - Mon (8am)

WEST VIRGINIA

Charleston - *Kanawha County*
Animal Emergency Clinic
5304 Maccorkle Avenue
Charleston, WV 25309
Phone: (304) 768-2911
Fax: (304) 768-6991
Website: --
Hours: 24 hours a day;
       7 days a week;
       365 days a year

Fairmont - *Marion County*
North Central West Virginia
   Vet Emergency
Interstate 79/Route 336 (Exit 139)
Fairmont, WV 26554
Phone: (304) 363-2227
Fax: --
Website: --
Hours: Mon - Fri (6pm-7:30am);
      Weekends from Sat (1pm) -
      Mon (7:30am)

Parkersburg - *Wood County*
Animal Veterinary
   Emergency Treatment
3602 East 7th Street - Suite B
Parkersburg, WV 26104
Phone: (304) 428-8387
Fax: --
Website: --
Hours: Call for current
      emergency hours.

Wheeling - *Ohio County*
Animal Urgent Care, Inc.
4201 Wood Street
Wheeling, WV 26003
Phone: (304) 233-0002
Fax: (304) 233-0052
Website: --
Hours: Call for current
      emergency hours.

Town & Country Animal Hospital
831 Old Fairmont Pike
Wheeling, WV 26003
Phone: (304) 242-9575
Fax: --
Website:
www.townandcountryanimalhospital.com
Hours: 24 hours a day; 7 days a week
Note: Daytime practice also at
      this location.

Zepol and Cher

WISCONSIN

Appleton - *Outagamie County*
Fox Valley Animal Referral Center
4706 New Horizons Boulevard
Appleton, WI 54914
Phone: (920) 993-9193
Fax: --
Website: www.fvarc.com
Hours: 24 hours a day;
7 days a week;
365 days a year

Glendale - *Monroe County*
Animal Emergency Center
2100 West Silver Spring Drive
Glendale, WI 53209
Phone: (414) 540-6710
Fax: (414) 540-6720
Website:
www.animalemergencycenter.com
Hours: 24 hours a day;
7 days a week;
365 days a year

Green Bay - *Brown County*
Green Bay Animal Emergency Center
933 Anderson Drive - Suite F
Green Bay, WI 54304
Phone: (920) 494-9400
Fax: --
Website: www.gbaec.com
Hours: Weeknights (6pm-8am);
Weekends & Holidays 24 Hrs

Ivan and dog park friend

MADISON - *Dane County*
University of Wisconsin - Madison
Veterinary Medical Teaching Hospital
2015 Linden Drive
Madison, WI 53706
Phone: (608) 263-7600
Toll Free: (800) DVM-VMTH
Website: www.vetmed.wisc.edu
Hours: By appointment Mon - Fri
(9am-5pm).
Note: At the time of this writing,
24 hour emergency service
is available on a case by
case basis. Must call to
discuss first.

Madison - *Dane County*
Emergency Clinic For Animals S.C.
229 West Beltline Highway
Madison, WI 53713
Phone: (608) 274-7772
Fax: --
Website:
www.emergencyclinicforanimals.com
Hours: 24 hours a day;
7 days a week;
365 days a year

Middleton - *Dane County*
Veterinary Emergency Service (VES)
1612 North High Point Road
Middleton, WI 53562
Phone: (608) 831-1101
Fax: --
Website:
www.veterinaryemergencyservice.com
Hours: 24 hours a day; 7 days a week

Milwaukee - *Milwaukee County*
Refer to Glendale

(Wisconsin continues)

WISCONSIN (continued)

Mosinee - *Marathon County*
Emergency Vets Of Central Wisconsin
1420 Kronenwetter Drive
Mosinee, WI 54455
Phone: (715) 693-6934
Fax: --
Website: --
Hours: Mon - Thurs (5pm-8am);
      Weekends from Fri (5pm) -
      Mon (8am); Holidays

Waukesha - *Waukesha County*
Wisconsin Veterinary Referral Center
  (WVRC)
360 Bluemound Road
Waukesha, WI, 53188
Phone: (262) 542-3241
Toll Free: (866) 542-3241
Fax: (262) 542-0805
Website: www.wivrc.com
Hours: 24 hours a day; 7 days a week

Dawn

WYOMING

Casper - *Natrona County*

The following facilities rotate emergencies days, nights, and weekends. Call Animal Hospital of Casper (or the other hospitals) and they will advise who is open the time you plan to visit.

1) Animal Hospital of Casper
2060 Fairgrounds Road
Casper, WY 82604
Phone: (307) 266-1660
Fax: (307) 266-1665
Website: www.petdrs.com
Hours: Rotational

2) All Creatures Veterinary Hospital
4590 East Yellowstone Highway
Evansville, WY 82636
Phone: (307) 235-2884
Fax: --
Website: --
Hours: Rotational

3) Ark Animal Hospital
4171 Swingle Acres Road
Casper, WY 82604
Phone: (307) 577-7387
Fax: --
Website: --
Hours: Rotational

4) Best Friends Animal Health Center
3163 Prospector Drive
Casper, WY 82604
Phone: (307) 235-4889
Fax: (307) 235-5646
Website:
    www.casperbestfriends.com
Hours: Rotational

Jackson - *Teton County*
Animal Care Clinic of Jackson
415 East Pearl Avenue
Jackson, WY 83001
Phone: (307) 733-5590
Fax: --
Website: --
Hours: 24 Hr Emergency Service

Zephyr

Pet E.R. Guide

Chapter Three

Veterinary Teaching Hospitals

Special Assistance for Your Pet

Chapter Three

Veterinary Teaching Hospitals
SPECIAL ASSISTANCE FOR YOUR PET

Throughout the United States there are many Veterinary Medicine Teaching Hospitals. These hospitals train the veterinarians that we depend on to care for our pets. This section lists those universities and veterinary colleges that have extensive Veterinary Medicine programs for their students, patients, and pet parents too.

You will note that the information contained in this section relates to companion animals as well as larger animals. If I were reading this, I would probably ask 'Why include large animals?' But, after our own recent stay at a lovely state park, we became aware of the number of people who traveled and camped with their horses. It was absolutely lovely to see this equestrian camping facility on the grounds. Having seen dogs, cats, birds, and other pets in our travels, it became apparent that no matter the size of the animal they would be a part of our 'family' too. Thus, they have been included in this broader University Medicine category, and this chapter.

Should your animal have a need for specialized medical attention while on the road, you will want to be aware of these facilities, in addition to any need for emergency care. For those pets that have special needs and still travel with their family, these facilities may well be facilities your home veterinarian may want to refer you to for continued care on the road. Please make sure your veterinarian makes the referral, preferably, before your travels begin.

Some facilities are open to all emergencies; others are open only if appointments have been made in advance; and others are available when a referral has been requested from the 'home' veterinarian. Each veterinary college has its own procedures which, like any business, can change periodically. Therefore, it is always beneficial to investigate what the school's current animal treatment policy is. Additionally, unique circumstances that a pet may be experiencing, while you are traveling, could generate an exception to their general policy. It is always worth the effort of an inquiry, especially when in doubt.

Note: These Universities are also included in Chapter Two along with the after-hour clinics. They are identifiable in Chapter Two by the town/city name being listed in capital letters and in bold.

ALABAMA

AUBURN UNIVERSITY
College of Veterinary Medicine
1185 Wire Road
Auburn University, AL 36849
Website: www.vetmed.auburn.edu
Small & Large Animal Hospital
Phone: (334) 844-4690
* Scheduled appointments are available to residents within a specified mileage range.
* Scheduled appointments are available to residents beyond the specified mileage range with a referral from the primary veterinarian only.
* Emergency services are available with requirements.
* Please call.

TUSKEGEE UNIVERSITY
College of Veterinary Medicine, Nursing & Allied Health
Veterinary Teaching Hospital
Tuskegee University
Tuskegee, AL 36088
Website: www.tuskegee.edu
Main Phone: (344) 727-8174
Teaching Hospital Phone:
    (334) 727-8436
Fax: (334) 727-8177
* Scheduled appointments are available.
* Emergency services are available 24 hours a day.
* Please call.

CALIFORNIA

UNIVERSITY OF CALIFORNIA - DAVIS
School of Veterinary Medicine
William R. Pritchard Veterinary
    Medical Teaching Hospital
Garrod Drive
Davis, CA 95616
Website: www.vetmed.ucdavis.edu
Small Animal Clinic
Main Phone: (530) 752-1393
Emergency Phone: (530) 752-0186
Fax: (530) 752-9620
* Scheduled appointments are available.
* Emergency services are available.
* There is 24 hour critical care available.
* Please call.
Large Animal Clinic
Main Phone: (530) 752-0290
Emergency Phone: (530) 752-5438
Fax: (530) 752-9815
* Scheduled appointments are available.
* Emergency services are available 24 hours a day.
* Please call.

COLORADO

COLORADO STATE UNIVERSITY
College of Veterinary Medicine
Biomedical Sciences
James L. Voss Veterinary
  Teaching Hospital
300 West Drake Road
Fort Collins, CO 80523
Website: www.cvmbs.colostate.edu
Small and Large Animals
Phone: (970) 221-4535
Fax: (970) 297-4100
- Scheduled appointments are available.
- Emergency services are available 24 hours a day.
- Please call.

FLORIDA

UNIVERSITY OF FLORIDA
Veterinary Medical Center
2015 SW 16th Avenue
Gainesville, FL 32610
Website: www.vetmed.ufl.edu
Small Animal Hospital
Phone: (352) 392-2235
- Scheduled appointments are available.
- Small Animal Hospital is available to regular clients or those with a referral only.
- Please call.
Large Animal Hospital
Phone: (352) 392-2229
- Scheduled appointments are available.
- Large Animal Hospital is open 24 hours for emergency situations.
- Please call.

GEORGIA

UNIVERSITY OF GEORGIA
College of Veterinary Medicine
Carlton Street
Athens, GA 30602
Website: www.vet.uga.edu
Hospital Main Phone: (706) 542-3221
Small Animal Hospital
Phone: (706) 542-2895 or
  (800) 542-9294
Referral Fax: (706) 542-4701 or
  542-2858
- Scheduled appointments are available to residents within a specified mileage range.
- Scheduled appointments are available to residents beyond the specified mileage range with a referral from the primary veterinarian only.
- Emergency services are available 24 hours a day.
- Please call to discuss before coming to hospital.
Large Animal Hospital
Phone: (706) 542-3223
Referral Fax: (706) 542-4701
- Scheduled appointments are available.
- Emergency services are available 24 hours a day.
- Veterinary field calls are available depending on distance to location.
- Please call.

ILLINOIS

UNIVERSITY OF ILLINOIS
Veterinary Teaching Hospital
Small Animal Clinic (#1008)
Large Animal Clinic (#1102)
1008 & 1102 West Hazelwood Drive
Urbana, IL 61802
Website: www.cvm.uiuc.edu
Small Animal Clinic
Phone: (217) 333-5300
- Scheduled appointments are available.
- Emergency services are available 24 hours a day.
- Please call.

Large Animal Clinic
Phone: (217) 333-2000
- Scheduled appointments are available.
- Emergency services are available 24 hours a day.
- Please call.

INDIANA

PURDUE UNIVERSITY
Veterinary Teaching Hospital (VTH)
625 Harrison Street
West Lafayette, IN 47907
Website: www.vet.purdue.edu
Main Phone: (765) 494-7607
Small Animal Clinic
Phone: (765) 494-1107
- Scheduled appointments available with a referral only, as of this writing.

Large Animal Clinic
Phone: (765) 494-8548
- Call to discuss scheduled appointments and emergency care.
- No referral needed.

IOWA

IOWA STATE UNIVERSITY
College of Veterinary Medicine
South 16th Street
Ames, IA 50010
Website: www.vetmed.iastate.edu
Small Animal Hospital
Phone: (515) 294-4900
Fax: (515) 294-7520
- Scheduled appointments are available.
- Emergency services are available.
- Referrals are requested to come with pet's medical file history.
- Please call.

Large Animal Hospital
Phone: (515) 294-1500
Fax: (515) 294-5224
- Scheduled appointments are available.
- Facility is staffed 24 hours a day, 365 days a year.

KANSAS

KANSAS STATE UNIVERSITY
College of Veterinary Medicine
Denison Avenue
Manhattan, KS 66506
Website: www.vet.ksu.edu
Small Animal & Exotics
Phone: (785) 532-5690
- Scheduled appointments are available.
- Emergency services are available 24 hours a day.
- Please call.

Large Animal/Equine and Agricultural
Phone: (785) 532-5700
- Scheduled appointments are available.
- Emergency services are available 24 hours a day.
- Please call.

LOUISANA

LOUISIANA STATE UNIVERSITY
LSU School of
Veterinary Medicine
Skip Bertman Drive
Baton Rouge, LA 70803
Website: www.vetmed.lsu.edu
Main Phone: (225) 578-9592
Fax: (225) 578-9559
<u>Small Animal</u>
Emergency Phone: (225) 578-9600
- Scheduled appointments are available.
- Referrals are requested to come with pet's medical file history.
- Emergency services are available 24 hours a day.
- Please call.

Note: Exotic pets and avian emergencies seen by medical practitioner 'on call' for these pets.

<u>Large Animal</u>
Emergency Phone: (225) 578-9500
- Scheduled appointments are available.
- Referrals are requested to come with pet's medical file history.
- Emergency services are available 24 hours a day.
- Please call.

MASSACHUSETTS

TUFTS UNIVERSITY
Cummings School of
Veterinary Medicine
200 Westboro Road
North Grafton, MA 01536
Website: www.tufts.edu/vet
<u>Small and Large Animal</u>
Phone: (508) 839-5302
Main Hospital: (508) 839-5395
Emergency Services: (508) 839-5395
Hospital Fax: (508) 839-7951
- Scheduled appointments are available.
- Emergency services are available 24 hours a day.
- Please call.

MICHIGAN

MICHIGAN STATE UNIVERSITY
College of Veterinary Medicine
Vet Med Center
East Lansing, MI 48824-1314
Website: www.cvm.msu.edu
Phone: (517) 353-4523 Main
<u>Small Animal Emergency</u>
Phone: (517) 353-5420
- Scheduled appointments are available with a referral from the primary veterinarian.
- Emergency services are available 24 hours a day.
- Please call.

<u>Large Animal Emergency</u>
Phone: (517) 353-9710
Fax: (517) 432-4091
- Scheduled appointments are available with a referral from the primary veterinarian.
- Emergency services are available 24 hours a day.
- Please call.

MINNESOTA

UNIVERSITY OF MINNESOTA
Veterinary Medical Center (VMC)
1365 Gortner Avenue
St. Paul, MN 55108
Website: www.cvm.umn.edu
Small Animal Hospital
Phone: (612) 626-VETS (8387)
- Scheduled appointments are available.
- Emergency services are available 24 hours a day.
- Please call.

Note: Facility is staffed 24 hours a day, everyday.

Large Animal Hospital
Phone: (612) 625-6700
- Scheduled appointments are available.
- Emergency services are available 24 hours a day.
- Please call.

Note: Facility is staffed 24 hours a day, everyday.

Emergency Services
Phone: (612) 625-9711
- Emergency services are available 24 hours a day.
- Please call.

Note: Facility is staffed 24 hours a day, everyday.

MISSISSIPPI

MISSISSIPPI STATE UNIVERSITY
College of Veterinary Medicine
Mississippi State, MS 39762
Website: www.cvm.msstate.edu
Appointment Phone: (662) 325-1351
Emergency Phone: (662) 325-3432
Fax: (662) 325-4596
- Scheduled appointments are available.
- Emergency services are available 24 hours a day.
- Please call.

MISSOURI

UNIVERSITY OF MISSOURI
College of Veterinary Medicine
Veterinary Medical Teaching Hospital
Clydesdale Hall
Columbia, MO 65211
Website: www.cvm.missouri.edu
Small Animal
Phone: (573) 882-7821
Emergency Phone: (573) 882-4589
Fax: (573) 884-5444
- Scheduled appointments are available.
- Emergency services are available 24 hours a day.
- Please call.

Large Animal
Phone: (573) 882-3513
Emergency Phone: (573) 882-4589
Fax: (573) 884-0173
- Emergency services are available 24 hours a day. Must call emergency number and a veterinarian will return the call.

NEW YORK

CORNELL UNIVERSITY
College of Veterinary Medicine
Campus Road
Ithaca, NY 14853
Website: www.vet.cornell.edu
Small Animal
Phone: (607) 253-3060
- Scheduled appointments are available.
- Emergency services are available 24 hours a day.
- Please call.

Note: There is a special exotic clinic for ferrets, rabbits, rodents, birds, and reptiles providing emergency and 24 hour service.

Equine & Farm Animal
Phone: (607) 253-3100
- Scheduled appointments are available.
- Emergency services are available 24 hours a day.
- Please call.

NORTH CAROLINA

NORTH CAROLINA STATE UNIVERSITY
College of Veterinary Medicine
Veterinary Teaching Hospital (VTH)
4700 Hillsborough Street
Raleigh, NC 27606
Website: www.cvm.ncsu.edu
Small Animal
Hospital Phone: (919) 513-6670
Hospital Fax: (919) 513-6713
- Scheduled appointments are available.
Emergency Phone: (919) 513-6911
Emergency Fax: (919) 513-6225
- Hours: Mon - Thurs (5pm - 8am); Weekends Fri (5pm) - Mon (8am); Holidays
- No referrals are needed during those hours. Always call first.

Large Animal
Main Phone: (919) 513-6640
After Hours Phone: (919) 513-6500
Fax: (919) 513-6717
- Large Animals are seen by the hospital with or without a referral 24 hours a day.

OHIO

THE OHIO STATE UNIVERSITY
College of Veterinary Medicine
1900 Coffey Road
Columbus, OH 43210
Website: www.vet.ohio-state.edu
Small Animal Hospital
Phone: (614) 292-3551
- Scheduled appointments are available.
- Emergency services are available.
- Please call for hospital's emergency hours.

Large Animal
Phone: (614) 292-6661
- Scheduled appointments are available.
- Emergency services are available 24 hours a day.
- Please call.

OKLAHOMA

OKLAHOMA STATE UNIVERSITY
Center for Veterinary Health Sciences
Stillwater, OK 74708
Website: www.cvm.okstate.edu
Phone: (405) 744-7000
Option 1: Small Animal Clinic
Option 2: Large Animal Clinic
Option 3: Other areas of Veterinary Teaching Hospital (VTH)
- Scheduled appointments are available.
- Emergency services are available 24 hours a day.
- Please call.

OREGON

OREGON STATE UNIVERSITY
Lois Bates Acheson Veterinary Teaching Hospital
SW 30th Street
Corvallis, OR 97331
Website: www.oregonstate.edu/vetmed
Small Animal
Phone 1: (541) 737-4812
Phone 2: (541) 737-4813
- Scheduled appointments are available with a referral from the primary veterinarian.
- As of this writing, there is no emergency care for animals unless they are a current patient.

Large Animal
Phone: (541) 737-2858
- Please call for current services available.

PENNSYLVANNIA

UNIVERSITY OF PENNSYLVANIA
Matthew J. Ryan Veterinary Hospital

Small Animals

39th & Spruce Streets

Philadelphia, PA

Website: www.vet.upenn.edu

Appointment Phone:
  (215) 746-VETS (215) 746-8387

Emergency Phone:
  (215) 746-V911 (215) 746-8911

- Scheduled appointments are available.
- Emergency services are available 24 hours a day.
- Please call.

George D. Widener Hospital for Large Animals

Large Animals

New Bolton Center

382 West Street Road

Kennett Square, PA 19348

Website: www.vet.upenn.edu

Emergency & Main Phone:
  (610) 444-5800 or 925-6525

Referring Veterinarians:
  1-877-PENNVET

- Call for services available.

TENNESSEE

UNIVERSITY OF TENNESSEE
College of Veterinary Medicine

2407 River Drive

Knoxville, TN 37996

Website: www.vet.utk.edu

Small Animal Clinical Sciences

Phone: (865) 974-8387 (VETS)

- Scheduled appointments are available with a referral from the primary veterinarian.
- Emergency services are available 24 hours a day.
- Please call.

Large Animal Clinic

Phone: (865) 974-5701 or 5702

- Scheduled appointments available with or without a referral.
- Call for other services.

Avian & Exotic Animal Clinic

Phone: (865) 974-8387

- Scheduled appointments available with or without a referral.
- Call for services offered.

TEXAS

TEXAS A&M UNIVERSITY
Veterinary Medical
Teaching Hospital
University Drive
College Station, TX 77843
Website: www.cvm.tamu.edu
Small Animal
Local Clientele Appointment Phone:
(979) 845-9062
Referral Appointment Phone:
(979) 845-2095
Emergency Phone: (979) 845-2351
- Scheduled appointments are available.
- Emergency services are available 24 hours a day. Must call before arriving.

Exotic Animals
Phone: (979) 845-4300
- Scheduled appointments are available.
- Emergency services are available 24 hours a day. Must call before arriving.

Large Animal
Phone: (979) 845-3541 for Appointments and Emergencies
Phone: (979) 845-9135 Field Services
Fax: (979) 845-6226
- Scheduled appointments are available.
- Emergency services are available 24 hours a day. Must call before arriving.

VIRGINIA

VIRGINIA TECH AND UNIVERSITY OF MARYLAND
Virginia-Maryland Regional
College of Veterinary Medicine
(VMRCVM)
Virginia Tech, Duck Pond Drive
Blacksburg, VA 24061
Website: www.vetmed.vt.edu
Phone: (540) 231-7666
Hospital Fax: (540) 231-9354
Small Animal Services
Phone: (540) 231-4621
- Scheduled appointments available to residents within a specified mileage range.
- Scheduled appointments available to residents beyond the specified mileage range with a referral from the primary veterinarian only.
- Emergency services are available on a case by case basis. Please call.

Equine Field Services
Phone: (540) 321-9042
Large Animal Services
- Scheduled appointments are available.
- Emergencies handled 24 hours a day.
- Field services are available daily.

WASHINGTON

WASHINGTON STATE UNIVERSITY
Veterinary Teaching Hospital
NE Grimes Way
Pullman, WA 99164
Website: www.vetmed.wsu.edu
Phone: (509) 335-0711
Small Animal Appointment
  Phone 1: (509) 335-0751
  Phone 2: (509) 335-0752
  Phone 3: (509) 335-0711
Large Animal Service Phone:
  (509) 335-0711
  • Scheduled appointments are available.
  • Emergency services are available 24 hours a day for both small and large animals. Call before arriving.

WISCONSIN

UNIVERSITY OF WISCONSIN - MADISON
Veterinary Medical Teaching Hospital
2015 Linden Drive
Madison, WI 53706
Website: www.vetmed.wisc.edu
Phone: (608) 263-7600 or
  1-800-DVM-VMTH
Small Animal Services
  • Scheduled appointments available.
  • Emergency services are available to referrals or returning patients.
Large Animal Services
  • Scheduled appointments available.
  • Emergency service can be arranged anytime. Call number above.

Pet E.R. Guide

Chapter Four

Keep Your Pets Safe

Ten Most Common Poisonous Plants

Toxic and Non-toxic Plant Lists

'A Poison Safe Home'

Reprinted with the permission of The American Society for the Prevention of Cruelty to Animals (ASPCA).

Chapter Four

Animal Poison Emergency

As a pet owner it is always our intent to keep our pets safe and healthy but, sometimes things do happen. The American Society for the Prevention of Cruelty to Animals (ASPCA) has their Animal Poison Control Center (APCC) which has assisted animal owners and veterinarians for years.

And, as such, it is with gratefulness and gratitude that we are able to share with you, with permission from the American Society for the Prevention of Cruelty to Animals (ASPCA), this section and some quick reference guides.

"As the premier animal poison control center in North America, the APCC is your best resource for any animal poison-related emergency, 24 hours a day, 365 days a year. If you think that your pet may have ingested a potentially poisonous substance, make the call that can make all the difference: **(888) 426-4435.** A $55 consultation fee may be applied to your credit card."

Ten Most Common Poisonous Plants

Marijuana

Ingestion of *Cannabis sativa* by companion animals can result in depression of the central nervous system and incoordination, as well as vomiting, diarrhea, drooling, increased heart rate, and even seizures and coma.

Sago Palm

All parts of *Cycas Revoluta* are poisonous, but the seeds or "nuts" contain the largest amount of toxin. The ingestion of just one or two seeds can result in very serious effects, which include vomiting, diarrhea, depression, seizures and liver failure.

Lilies

Members of the *Lilium spp.* are considered to be highly toxic to cats. While the poisonous component has not yet been identified, it is clear that with even ingestions of very small amounts of the plant, severe kidney damage could result.

Tulip/Narcissus Bulbs

The bulb portions of *Tulipa/ Narcissus spp.* contain toxins that can cause intense gastrointestinal irritation, drooling, loss of appetite, depression of the central nervous system, convulsions and cardiac abnormalities.

Ten Most Common Poisonous Plants (continued)

Azalea/Rhododendron

Members of the *Rhododenron spp.* contain substances known as grayantoxins, which can produce vomiting, drooling, diarrhea, weakness and depression of the central nervous system in animals. Severe azalea poisoning could ultimately lead to coma and death from cardiovascular collapse.

Oleander

All parts of *Nerium oleander* are considered to be toxic, as they contain cardiac glycosides that have the potential to cause serious effects—including gastrointestinal tract irritation, abnormal heart function, hypothermia and even death.

Castor Bean

The poisonous principle in *Ricinus communis* is ricin, a highly toxic protein that can produce severe abdominal pain, drooling, vomiting, diarrhea, excessive thirst, weakness and loss of appetite. Severe cases of poisoning can result in dehydration, muscle twitching, tremors, seizures, coma and death.

Cyclamen

Cyclamen species contain cyclamine, but the highest concentration of this toxic component is typically located in the root portion of the plant. If consumed, *Cylamen* can produce significant gastrointestinal irritation, including intense vomiting. Fatalities have also been reported in some cases.

Kalanchoe

This plant contains components that can produce gastrointestinal irritation, as well as those that are toxic to the heart, and can seriously affect cardiac rhythm and rate.

Yew

Taxus spp. contains a toxic component known as taxine, which causes central nervous system effects such as trembling, incoordination, and difficulty breathing. It can also cause significant gastrointestinal irritation and cardiac failure, which can result in death.

Toxic Plants

This list contains plants that have been reported as having systemic effects on animals and/or intense effects on the gastrointestinal tract.

Please note that the information contained in our plant lists is not meant to be all-inclusive, but rather a compilation of the most frequently encountered plants. For more information, contact us at napcc@aspca.org.

A

Aloe
Amaryllis
Andromeda Japonica
Asian Lily (*Liliaceae*)
Asparagus Fern
Australian Nut
Autumn Crocus
Avocado
Azalea

B

Bird of Paradise
American Bittersweet
European Bittersweet
Branching Ivy
Buckeye
Buddist Pine

C

Caladium
Calla Lily
Castor Bean
Ceriman (aka Cutleaf Philodendron)
Charming Diffenbachia
Chinaberry Tree
Chinese Evergreen
Christmas Rose
Clematis
Cordatum
Corn Plant (aka Cornstalk Plant)
Cornstalk Plant (aka Corn Plant)
Cutleaf Philodendron (aka Ceriman)
Cycads
Cyclamen

D

Daffodil
Day Lily
Devil's Ivy
Dumb Cane
Deadly Nightshade (See Nightshade)

E

Easter Lily
Elephant Ears
Emerald Feather (aka Emerald Fern)
Emerald Fern (aka Emerald Feather)
English Ivy

F

Fiddle-Leaf Philodendron
Flamingo Plant
Florida Beauty
Foxglove
Fruit Salad Plant

G

Glacier Ivy
Gladiolas
Glory Lily
Gold Dieffenbachia
Gold Dust Dracaena
Golden Pothos
Green Gold Nephthysis

H

Hahn's self branching English Ivy
Heartleaf Philodendron
Heavenly Bamboo
Holly
Horsehead Philodendron

Hurricane Plant
Hyacinth
Hydrangea

I

Iris

J

Japanese Show Lily
Japanese Yew (aka Yew)
Jerusalem Cherry

K

Kalanchoe

L

Lace Fern
Lacy Tree
Lily of the Valley

M

Macadamia Nut
Madagascar Dragon Tree
Marble Queen
Marijuana
Mauna Loa Peace Lily (aka Peace Lily)
Mexican Breadfruit
Mistletoe "American"
Morning Glory
Mother-in-Law

N

Narcissus
Needlepoint Ivy
Nephthytis
Nightshade

O

Oleander
Onion
Orange Day Lily

P

Panda
Peace Lily (aka Mauna Loa Peace Lily)
Philodendron Pertusum

Plumosa Fern
Precatory Bean

Q

Queensland Nut

R

Red Emerald
Red Lily
Red-Margined Dracaena
    (aka Straight-Margined Dracaena)
Red Princess
Rhododendron
Ribbon Plant (*Dracaena sanderiana*)
Rubrum Lily

S

Saddle Leaf Philodendron
Sago Palm
Satin Pothos
Schefflera
Spotted Dumb Cane
Stargazer Lily
Striped Dracaena
Sweetheart Ivy
Swiss Cheese Plant

T

Taro Vine
Tiger Lily
Tomato Plant
Tree Philodendron
Tropic Snow Dumbcane
Tulip

V

Variable Dieffenbachia
Variegated Philodendron

W

Warneckei Dracaena
Wood Lily

Y

Yesterday, Today, Tomorrow
Yew (aka Japanese Yew)
Yucca

Non-toxic Plants

This list contains plants that have not been reported as having systemic effects on animals or as having intense effects on the gastrointestinal tract. Any plant material ingested by an animal (as when dogs and cats ingest yard grass) may produce signs of vomiting, depression, or diarrhea. These signs are generally mild and self-limiting and often do not require any treatment.

Please note that the information contained in our plant lists is not meant to be all-inclusive, but rather a compilation of the most frequently encountered plants. For general information on plants not included on either list, please feel free to contact us at napcc@aspca.org.

A

Achira
Acorn Squash
African Violet
Algaroba
Aluminum Plant
Alumroot
American Rubber
Anthericum comosum
Antirrhinum multiform
Arabian Gentian
Aregelia
Artillery Plant
Aspidium falcatum
Autumn Olive

B

Bachelor's Buttons
Ball Fern
Bamboo
Bamboo Palm
Bamboo Vine
Banana
Banana Squash
Begonia Species
Belmore Sentry Palm
Big Shellbark Hickory
Bitter Pecan
Bitternut

Black Haw
Black Hawthorn
Blaspheme Vine
Bloodleaf
Blooming Sally
Bluebottle
Blue Bead
Blue Daisy
Blue Echeveria
Blue-dicks
Blue-eyed Daisy
Blunt Leaf Peperomia
Blushing Bromeliad
Bold Sword Fern
Boston Fern
Bottlebrush
Bottle Palm
Brazilian Orchid
Bride's Bonnet
Bristly Greenbrier
Broom Hickory
Brodiaea pulchella
Bullbrier
Butterfly Ginger
Butterfly Iris
Bur Gourd
Burro's Tail
Buttercup Squash
Butterfly Squash

C

Calathea insignis
Calthea lancifolia
California Pitcher Plant
Callistemon bradyandrus
Callistemon viminalis
Callistemon citrinus
Calochortus nuttalli
Camellia
Canada Hemlock
Canary Date Palm
Candle Plant
Candycorn Plant
Canna Lily
Cantebury-bell
Cape Jasmine
Cape Primrose
Carob
Carob Tree
Caroba
Carobinha
Carolina Hemlock
Carrion Flower
Carrot Flower
Carrot Fern
Casaba Melon
Cast Iron Plant
Cat Brier
Cat Ear
Cattleya labiata
Celosia globosa
Celosia plumosa
Celosia spicata
Chamaedorean
Chaparral
Chenille Plant
Chestnut
Chicken-gizzard
Chickens and Hens
Chin-lao-shu
China Aster
China Root
Chinese Plumbago
Chlorophytum

Chlorophytum bechetii
Chocolate Soldier
Christmas Dagger
Christmas Palm
Christmas Orchid
Cinnamon
Cinquefoil
Cirrhopetalum
Clearweed
Cliff Brake
Cocks Comb
Cocktail Orchid
Collinia elegans
Color-Band
Columnar
Common Camellia
Common Catbrier
Common Garden Canna
Common Greenbrier
Common Snapdragon
Common Staghorn Fern
Confederate Jasmine
Coolwort
Copperlead
Copper Rose
Coral Ardisia
Coral Bells
Coralberry
Cornflower
Crape Myrtle
Creeping Charlie
Creeping Gloxinia
Creeping Mahonia
Creeping Pilea
Creeping Rubus
Creeping Zinnia
Crepe Myrtle
Crimson Bottlebush
Crimson Cup
Crisped Feather Fern
Crossandra
Cucumber
Cushon Aloe
Cushion Moss
Cyrtudeira reptans

D

Dainty
Dainty Rabbits-foot Fern
Dallas Fern
Dancing Doll Orchid
Davallia bullata mariessi
Davallia trichomanoides
Desert Trumpet
Dichelostemma
Dichorisandra reginae
Dinteranthus vanzylii
Duffii Fern
Duffy Fern
Dwarf Date Palm
Dwarf Feather Fern
Dwarf Palm
Dwarf Rose-stripe Star
Dwarf Royal Palm
Dwarf Whitman Fern

E

Earth Star
Easter Cattleya
Easter Daisy
Easter Lily Cactus
Easter Orchid
Edible Banana
Elephant-Ear Begonia
Emerald Ripple Peperomia
English Hawthorn
Epidendrum atropurpeum
Epidendrum ibaguense
Epidendrum
Episcia spp.

F

False Aralia
Fairy Fountain
Fan Tufted Palm
Feather Fern
Feathered Amaranth
Fiery Reed Orchid
Figleaf Gourd
Figleaf Palm

Fingernail Plant
Fire Weed
Fish Tail Fern
Flame African Violet
Flame of the Woods
Flame Violet
Florida Butter-fly Orchid
Fluffy Ruffles
Forster Sentry Palm
Fortunes Palm
Freckle Face
Friendship Plant
Frosty

G

Garden Marigold
Garden Snapdragon
German Violet
Gherkins
Ghost Leafless Orchid
Ghost Plant
Giant Aster
Giant Holly Fern
Giant White Inch Plant
Gibasis geniculata
Globe Thistle
Gloxinia
Gold Bloom
Gold-fish Plant
Golden Bells
Golden Lace Orchid
Golden Shower Orchid
Good Luck Palm
Grape Hyacinth
Grape Ivy
Great Willow Herb
Green Ripple Peperomia
Greenbrier

H

Hagbrier
Hardy Baby Tears
Hardy Gloxinia
Haws

Haws Apple
Haworthia
Hawthorn
Hedgehog Gourd
Hellfetter
Hemlock Tree
Hen and Chickens Fern
Hens and Chickens
Hickory
Hindu Rope Plant
Holligold
Holly Fern
Hollyhock
Honey Locust
Honey Plant
Honeydew Melons
Honeysuckle Fuchsia
Hookera pulchella
Horse Brier
Hoya carnosa 'exotica'
Hoya carnosa 'krinkle'
Hoya carnosa 'variegata'
Hoya 'Mauna Loa'
Hubbard Squash
Hypocyrta spp.

I

Ice Plant
Imbricata Sword Fern
Irish Moss
Iron Cross Begonia
Iron Tree
Ivy Peperomia
Ivy-leaf Peperomia

J

Jackson Brier
Jacob's Ladder
Japanese Aralia
Japanese Holly Fern
Japanese Moss
Japanese Pittosporum
Jasmine

Jewel Orchid
Joseph's Coat
Jungle Geranium

K

Kaempferia
Kahali Ginger
Kenilworth Ivy
Kentia Palm
Kenya Palm
Kenya Violet
Kharoub
King Nut
King of the Forest
King and Queen Fern
Kuang-yen-pa-hsieh

L

Lace Flower Vine
Lace Orchid
Ladies Ear Drops
Lady Lou
Lady Palm
Lagerstroemia indica
Lance Pleomele
Large Lady Palm
Laurel-leaved Greenbrier
Leather Peperomia
Leng-fen Tu'an
Leopard Lily
Leopard Orchid
Lesser Snapdragon
Lily of the Valley Orchid
Linden
Lipstick Plant
Little Zebra Plant
Little Fantasy Peperomia
Living Rock Cactus
Living Stones
Locust Pods
Lou-lang-t'ou
Luther

M

Madagascar Jasmine
Magnolia Bush
Mahonia aquifolium
Malabar Gourd
Malaysian Dracaena
Manila Palm
Mapleleaf Begonia
Maranta
Marbled Fingernail
Mariposa Lily
Maroon
Mary-bud
Measles Plant
Melons
Metallic Peperomia
Metallic Leaf Begonia
Mexican Firecracker
Mexican Rosettes
Mexican Snowballs
Miniature Date Palm
Minature Fish Tail
Minature Maranta
Minature Marble Plant
Mistletoe Cactus
Mockernut Hickory
Mosaic Plant
Moss Agate
Moss Campion
Moss Fern
Moss Phlox
Moss Rose
Mossy Campion
Mother Fern
Mother Spleenwort
Mother of Pearl
Mountain Camellia
Mountain Grape
Mulberry Bush Greenbrier
Mulberry Tree
Musa paradisiaca
Muscari armeniacum
Muscari spp.
Muskmellon

N

Narrow Leafed Pleomele
Natal Plum
Neanthe Bella Palm
Nematanthus spp.
Neoregelia
Nephrolepsis
Nerve Plant
New Silver and Bronze
Night Blooming Cereus

O

Odontoglossum spp.
Old Man Cactus
Old World Orchid
Orange Star
Oregon Grape

P

Paddy's Wig
Painted Lady
Palm Lily
Pampus Grass
Panamiga
Pansy Orchid
Paradise Palm
Parlor Palm
Parlor Plant
Parsley Fern
Peace Begonia
Peacock Plant
Pearl Plant
Pearly Dots
Peperomia hederifolia
Peperomia peltifolia
Peperomia rotundifolia
Peperomia sandersii
Pepper Face
Persian Violet
Pheasant Plant
Piggy Back Plant
Pigmy Date Palm
Pignut
Pignut Hickory

Pilea microphylla
Pilea mucosa
Pink Brocade
Pink Pearl
Pink Polka Dot Plant
Pink Starlite
Pirliteiro
Pitaya
Plantanus orientalis
Plantanus occidentalis
Platinum Peperomia
Platycerium alicicorne
Plumbago larpentiae
Plush Plant
Polka Dot Plant
Polystichum falcatum
Pony Tail
Porcelain Flower
Pot Marigold
Prairie Lily
Prairie Snowball
Prayer Plant
Prickly Bottlebrush
Prostrate Coleus
Purple Baby Tears
Purple Passion Vine
Purple Waffle Plant
Purpleosier Willow

Q

Queen's Spiderwort
Queencup
Queens Spiderwort
Queensland Arrowroot

R

Rabbit's Foot Fern
Rainbow Orchid
Red African Violet
Red Berried Greenbrier
Red Edge Peperomia
Red Hawthorne
Red Palm Lily
Red Veined Prayer
Reed Palm

Resurrection Lily
Rex Begonia
Rhynchophorum
Ribbon Plant (*Chlorophytum comosum*)
Roosevelt Fern
Royal Velvet Plant
Rubber Plant, Baby
Russian Olive

S

Saffron Spike Zebra
Saint Bernard's Lily
Sand Lily
Sand Verbena
Satin Pellionia
Sawbrier
Scabious
Scarborough Lily
Scarlet Orchid
Scarlet Sage
Sego Lily
Shagbark Hickory
Shan Ku'ei-lai
Shellbark Hickory
Shiny Leaf Smilax
Shrimp Cactus
Silver Bell
Silver Berry
Silver Heart
Silver-leaf Peperomia
Silver Nerve Plant
Silver Pink Vine
Silver Star
Silver Table Fern
Silver Tree Anamiga
Slender Deutzia
Small Fruited Hickory
Smilax tamnoides
Speckled Wood Lily
Spice Orchid
Spider Ivy
Spider Plant
Spotted Laurel
Squarenut

Squirrel's Foot Fern
Star Jasmine
Star Lily
Star Plant
Star Tulip
Star Window Plant
Strawberry
Striped Blushing
Sugar Pods
Sulfur Flower
Summer Hyacinth
Swedish Ivy
Sweetheart Hoya
Sweetheart Peperomia
Sweet William
Sword Fern

T

Tahitian Bridal Veil
Tailed Orchid
Tall Feather Fern
Tall Mahonia
Teasel Gourd
Texas Sage
Thea japonica
Thimble Cactus
Thorn Apple (*Carateagus oxyacanth*)
Ti Hu-ling
Tiger Orchid
Toad Spotted Cactus
Torch Lily
Tous-les-mois
Trailing Peperomia
Tree Cactus
Tree Gloxinia
Tropical Moss
True Cantalope
Tu Fu-ling
Tulip Poplar
Tulip Tree
Turban Squash
Turf Lily

U

Umbrella Plant
Urbinia agavoides
Usambara Violet

V

Variegated Laurel
Variegated Oval Leaf Peperomia
Variegated Wandering Jew
Variegated Wax Plant
Velvet Plant
Venus Fly Trap
Verona Fern
Verona Lace Fern
Vining Peperomia
Violet Slipper Gloxinia

W

Waffle Plant
Walking Anthericum
Washington Hawthorn
Water Hickory
Watermelon Begonia
Watermelon Peperomia
Watermelon Pilea
Wax Plant
Wax Rosette
Weeping Bottlebrush
Weeping Sergeant Hemlock
Weisdornbluten
West Indian Gherkin
Western Sword
White Ginger
White Edged Swedish Ivy
White Heart Hickory
Whitman Fern
Wild Buckwheat
Wild Hyacinth
Wild Lantana
Wild Sarsaparilla
Wild Strawberry
Willow Herb
Windmill Palm

Winter Cattleya
Withered Snapdragon
Woolflower

Y

Yellow Bloodleaf
Yellow-flowered Gourd
Yerba Linda

Z

Zebra Haworthia
Zebra Plant
Zinnia spp.
Zucchini Squash

A Poison Safe Home

Foods to Avoid Feeding Your Pet

Alcoholic beverages
Avocado
Chocolate (all forms)
Coffee (all forms)
Fatty foods
Macadamia nuts
Moldy or spoiled foods
Onions, onion powder
Raisins and grapes
Salt
Yeast dough
Garlic
Products sweetened with xylitol

Warm Weather Hazards

Animal toxins—toads, insects,
    spiders, snakes and scorpions
Blue-green algae in ponds
Citronella candles
Cocoa mulch
Compost piles
Fertilizers
Flea products
Outdoor plants and plant bulbs
Swimming-pool treatment supplies
Fly baits containing methomyl
Slug and snail baits containing
    metaldehyde

Medication

Common examples of human
medications that can be potentially
lethal to pets, even in small doses,
include:
    Pain killers
    Cold medicines
    Anti-cancer drugs
    Antidepressants
    Vitamins
    Diet Pills

Cold Weather Hazards

Antifreeze
Liquid potpourri
Ice melting products
Rat and mouse bait

Common Household Hazards

Fabric softener sheets
Mothballs
Post-1982 pennies (due to high
    concentration of zinc)

Holiday Hazards

Christmas tree water (may contain
    fertilizers and bacteria, which, if
    ingested, can upset the stomach)
Electrical cords
Ribbons or tinsel (can become
    lodged in the intestines and cause
    intestinal obstruction—most
    often occurs with kittens!)
Batteries
Glass ornaments

Non-toxic Substances for Dogs and Cats

The following substances are
considered to be non-toxic,
although they may cause mild
gastrointestinal upset in some
animals:
    Water-based paints
    Toilet bowl water
    Silica gel
    Poinsettia
    Cat litter
    Glue traps
    Glow jewelry

Pet E.R. Guide

Chapter Five

Emergency Travel & Evacuation

Chapter Five

Emergency Travel & Evacuation

You are probably asking yourself, why include information about emergency travel and evacuation in a guide book pertaining to Pet E.R.s?

Well, the answer is pretty simple. We would like you to be prepared to take care of your pets if there is a need to quickly leave your home or the area you are visiting. The best plan of action is to plan ahead. Being prepared will make an already difficult situation less difficult, and it will reduce stress for both you and your pets.

During the past few years we have had hurricanes, tornadoes, floods, wild fires, and other natural disasters throughout the country. During these events many people were asked to quickly move out of their area. Having known families who have gone through such evacuations, it can be stated that it is extremely stressful for both the people and the animals they care for. It generates a sense of urgency at a time when each moment may count towards a better result of safety. It is times such as these that being prepared can make an enormous difference. We hope that this section will help you prepare for and understand the options available to you and your pets in the event of an emergency evacuation.

We also encourage you to seek out state and federal publications on evacuation preparedness which provide useful instruction and advice. Additionally, animal related agencies and associations have wonderful reference guides available. The internet is always a good resource for finding this information.

There are also "veterinary approved" first aid and medical books, as well as first aid kits for your pets. Your veterinarian should be happy to provide you with their recommendation for these items.

We have listed some things that would be on our evacuation list. If you can think of more, please add them.

Exotic pets may have unique needs that you should discuss with your veterinarian, so tailor your list to your specific pet's needs.

For Planned Travel
Per Pet

Pet Identification Tag

An Ample Supply of Food

Can Opener (hand held type)

Spoons

An Ample, Clean Water Supply

Bowls/Dishes

Medications

Collar/Harness

Vaccination Tags

Leash

Crate/Kennel

Kitty Litter Box & Litter (cats)

Towel/Blanket

Pet Bed

Toy(s)

Photograph of Pet

Both In-state and Out-of-state Emergency Contacts (family member or friend)

Animal First Aid Kit (purchased kit or home-made with your veterinarian's input)

Certificate of Current Immunizations from Veterinarian

Documentation of Allergies or Other Important Medical Info

Medical Record History

Ownership Proof

Your Pet's Regular Veterinarian Information (Name, Address, Phone/Fax, Any other pertinent office info)

Veterinary Facility Info on the way to Destination

Veterinary Facility Info at Destination (Acquire emergency veterinary info for help on way and at destination)

"Poop Bags"

Microchipping or Tattooing your pet gives you and your pet a 'second chance' in the event of loss.

IMPORTANT: MAKE SURE YOUR PET IS REGISTERED AFTER MICROCHIPPING OR TATTOOING!

Planning is obviously important whether your travel is for business or pleasure. Traveling with pets takes extra effort, as many places do not accommodate pets in the best of circumstances. But if you are evacuating an area, time will be of the essence. You must prepare ahead of time to ensure the safety of your family and pets.

If you are evacuating to a hotel, research ahead of time whether or not your pets can remain with you. If you are evacuating to a shelter, realize that it is likely your pet is not going to be accepted into that shelter. If possible, call a boarding facility outside the affected evacuation area to see if they can care for your pet during your relocation. Many cities and states have evacuation plans that include the temporary boarding of animals. The pet and animal community is very supportive during times of crisis, and you will find assistance for both you and your pets. Check with local authorities for these locations and contact information.

Realize that if where you are isn't safe, it is not safe for your pets either.

We have pets because we love the companionship and closeness we have with them. They are a significant part of our family. As we travel, no matter where we go, we should always hold the interest of keeping all of our 'family members' happy, healthy, and safe.

We hope that you will find the Pet E.R. Guide a useful resource that will help you plan and care for your pets.

Happy Trails and Tails!

Pet E.R. Guide

Invitation

Regarding
Emergency Veterinarian Facilities

Please note that although we have tried to be comprehensive, it is likely that we have not included all of the emergency veterinary facilities in any particular area. If you are aware of, or work for, an emergency facility that is not included in this directory, please send us the following information to be reviewed for consideration:

Facility Name
Street Address
City/Town, State Zip Code
Phone Number
Fax Number
Email Address
Website Address
Hours Open

We would love to include these in a future release!

By the same token, if errors have been found or changes of information have occurred (a move of a location's facility, different phone numbers, names, or other changes), please let us know those as well. Our contact information appears on page 193, after the following index of locations.

Pet E.R. Guide

Index of Locations

Please note that any location in capital letters denotes a veterinary college hospital.

COLORADO

Loveland - Larimer County 42
Parker - Douglas County 42
Thornton - Adams County 43
Westminster - Adams County 43
Wheat Ridge - Jefferson County 43

CONNECTICUT

Bolton - Tolland County 44
Cheshire - New Haven County 44
Danbury - Fairfield County 44
Farmington - Hartford County 44
New Haven - New Haven County 44
Norwalk - Fairfield County 44
Oakdale-Montville -
   New London County 45
Rocky Hill - Hartford County 45
Shelton - Fairfield County 45
West Hartford - Hartford County 45

DELAWARE

Dover - Kent County 46
Newark - New Castle County 46
Wilmington - New Castle County 46

DISTRICT OF COLUMBIA

Washington, DC 47

FLORIDA

Boca Raton - Palm Beach County 48
Bradenton - Manatee County 48
Brandon - Hillsborough County 48
Casselberry - Seminole County 48
Clearwater - Pinellas County 49
Cooper City - Broward County 49
Coral Springs - Broward County 49
Daytona Beach - Volusia County 49
Deerfield Beach - Broward County 49
Estero - Lee County 50
Fort Myers - Lee County 50
Fort Pierce - St. Lucie County 50
GAINESVILLE -
   Alachua County 50, 152
Gainesville - Alachua County 50
Holly Hill - Volusia County 50

Hollywood - Broward County 51
Kendall - Miami-Dade County 51
Jacksonville -
   Duval/St. Johns County 51
Jacksonville Beach - Duval County 51
Jupiter - Palm Beach County 51
Lakeland - Polk County 51
Largo - Pinellas County 52
Leesburg - Lake County 52
Melbourne - Brevard County 52
Miami - Miami-Dade County 52
Naples - Collier County 52
Niceville - Okaloosa County 53
Ocala - Marion County 53
Orange Park - Clay County 53
Orlando - Orange County 53
Oviedo - Seminole County 53
Palm Beach Gardens -
   Palm Beach County 53
Palm Harbor - Pinellas County 54
Pembroke Pines - Broward County 54
Pensacola - Escambia County 54
Port Charlotte - Charlotte County 54
Port Richey - Pasco County 54
Rockledge - Brevard County 54
St. Augustine - St. Johns County 54
St. Petersburg - Pinellas County 55
Sarasota - Sarasota County 55
Spring Hill - Hernando County 55
Stuart - Martin County 55
Tallahassee - Leon County 55
Tampa - Hillsborough County 56
University Park - Manatee County 56
West Palm - Palm Beach County 56
Winter Park - Orange County 56

GEORGIA

Alpharetta - Fulton County 57
ATHENS - Clarke County 57, 152
Atlanta - Fulton County 57
Augusta -
   Augusta-Richmond County 57
Chamblee - DeKalb County 57
Columbus - Muscogee County 58

Baton Rouge -
   East Baton Rouge Parish 72
Lafayette - Lafayette Parish 72
Lake Charles - Calcasieu Parish 72
LaPlace -
   St. John the Baptist Parish 72
Mandeville - St. Tammany Parish 73
Metairie - Jefferson Parish 73
New Orleans - Jefferson Parish 73
Shreveport - Caddo Parish 73
Terrytown - Jefferson Parish 73
West Monroe - Ouachita Parish 73

MAINE

Brewer - Penobscot County 74
Lewiston - Androscoggin County 74
Portland - Cumberland County 74

MARYLAND

Annapolis - Anne Arundel County 75
Baltimore - Baltimore City 75
Bel Air - Harford County 75
Catonsville - Baltimore County 75
Ellicott City - Howard County 75
Frederick - Frederick County 75
Gaithersburg -
   Montgomery County 75
Glenn Dale -
   Prince George's County 76
Hyattstown - Montgomery County 76
Rockville - Montgomery County 76
Salisbury - Wicomico County 76
Urbana - Frederick County 76
Waldorf - Charles County 76
Westminster - Carroll County 76

MASSACHUSETTS

Acton - Middlesex County 77
Boston - Suffolk County 77
Buzzards Bay - Barnstable County 77
Hanover - Plymouth County 77
Nantucket - Nantucket County 77
North Andover - Essex County 77

NORTH GRAFTON -
   Worcester County 78, 154
Pittsfield - Berkshire County 78
South Deerfield - Franklin County 78
South Dennis - Barnstable County 78
Springfield - Hampden County 78
Swansea - Bristol County 78
Walpole - Norfolk County 78
Waltham - Middlesex County 79
West Bridgewater -
   Plymouth County 79
Weymouth - Norfolk County 79
Woburn - Middlesex County 79

MICHIGAN

Ann Arbor - Washtenaw County 80
Auburn Hills - Oakland County 80
Bloomfield Hills -
   Oakland County 80
Brighton - Livingston County 80
Clinton Township -
   Macomb County 80
Detroit - Wayne County 80
EAST LANSING -
   Ingham County 81, 154
Flint - Genesee County 81
Grand Rapids - Kent County 81
Harper Woods - Wayne County 81
Kalamazoo - Kalamazoo County 81
Lansing - Ingham County 81
Madison Heights -
   Oakland County 81
Milford - Oakland County 82
Novi - Oakland County 82
Plymouth - Wayne County 82
Rochester - Oakland County 82
Southfield - Oakland County 82
Southgate - Wayne County 82

MINNESOTA

Apple Valley - Dakota County 83
Coon Rapids - Anoka County 83
Duluth - St. Louis County 83
Eden Prairie - Hennepin County 83

UTAH

VERMONT

VIRGINIA

WASHINGTON

Pet E.R.
Guide

To update information currently included in the Pet E.R. Guide or to submit your 24- Hour or After Hours veterinarian facility:

Contact the author by:

Email
melinda@petemergencybook.com

Website
www.petemergencybook.com

To contact the publisher, Trailer Life Books, for product purchase/distribution or other general information:

Contact Trailer Life Books by:

Email
dbrown@affinitygroup.com

Website
www.TrailerLifeDirectory.com

Mail:
Trailer Life Books
2575 Vista Del Mar
Ventura, CA 93001
Attn: Debbie Brown

Phone:
1-800-765-7070 X512

Pet, Vet and Health Records
Please enter your pet's information here for
quick access in case of emergency.

Pet's Name:_____ ☐ Male ☐ Female

☐ Dog ☐ Cat ☐ Other:_____ Spayed/Neutered: ☐ Yes ☐ No

Primary Breed:_____ Age:_____

Primary Color(s):_____

Rabies Vaccination: ☐ Yes ☐ No Vaccination Date:_____/_____/_____ mo/dy/year

☐ Microchip ☐ Tattoo ID #:_____

Microchip   Company
Company Name:_____ Phone Number:_____

License Tag #:_____City/State Licensed In:_____

Veterinary Clinic:_____

Veterinarian's Name:_____

Veterinary Clinic Address:_____

City, State, ZIP:_____

Clinic Phone:_____Clinic Fax:_____

Current Medications:_____

Known Allergies:_____

Dietary Requirements:_____

History of Surgical Procedures, Injuries, or Treatments:

_____

_____

_____

_____

_____

_____

_____

Pet, Vet and Health Records
Please enter your pet's information here for
quick access in case of emergency.

Pet's Name:_____ ☐ Male ☐ Female

☐ Dog ☐ Cat ☐ Other:_____ Spayed/Neutered: ☐ Yes ☐ No

Primary Breed:_____ Age:_____

Primary Color(s):_____

Rabies Vaccination: ☐ Yes ☐ No Vaccination Date:_____/_____/_____ mo/dy/year

☐ Microchip ☐ Tattoo ID #:_____

Microchip   Company
Company Name:_____ Phone Number:_____

License Tag #:_____City/State Licensed In:_____

Veterinary Clinic:_____

Veterinarian's Name:_____

Veterinary Clinic Address:_____

City, State, ZIP:_____

Clinic Phone:_____Clinic Fax:_____

Current Medications:_____

Known Allergies:_____

Dietary Requirements:_____

History of Surgical Procedures, Injuries, or Treatments:

_____

_____

_____

_____

_____

_____

_____

Pet, Vet and Health Records
Please enter your pet's information here for quick access in case of emergency.

Pet's Name:_____ ☐ Male ☐ Female

☐ Dog ☐ Cat ☐ Other:_____ Spayed/Neutered: ☐ Yes ☐ No

Primary Breed:_____ Age:_____

Primary Color(s):_____

Rabies Vaccination: ☐ Yes ☐ No   Vaccination Date:_____/_____/_____ mo/dy/year

☐ Microchip ☐ Tattoo ID #:_____

Microchip   Company
Company Name:_____ Phone Number:_____

License Tag #:_____City/State Licensed In:_____

Veterinary Clinic:_____

Veterinarian's Name:_____

Veterinary Clinic Address:_____

City, State, ZIP:_____

Clinic Phone:_____Clinic Fax:_____

Current Medications:_____

Known Allergies:_____

Dietary Requirements:_____

History of Surgical Procedures, Injuries, or Treatments:

_____

_____

_____

_____

_____

_____

_____

Pet, Vet and Health Records
Please enter your pet's information here for
quick access in case of emergency.

Pet's Name:_____ ☐ Male ☐ Female

☐ Dog ☐ Cat ☐ Other:_____ Spayed/Neutered: ☐ Yes ☐ No

Primary Breed:_____ Age:_____

Primary Color(s):_____

Rabies Vaccination: ☐ Yes ☐ No Vaccination Date:_____/_____/_____ mo/dy/year

☐ Microchip ☐ Tattoo ID #:_____

Microchip   Company
Company Name:_____ Phone Number:_____

License Tag #:_____City/State Licensed In:_____

Veterinary Clinic:_____

Veterinarian's Name:_____

Veterinary Clinic Address:_____

City, State, ZIP:_____

Clinic Phone:_____Clinic Fax:_____

Current Medications:_____

Known Allergies:_____

Dietary Requirements:_____

History of Surgical Procedures, Injuries, or Treatments:

_____

_____

_____

_____

_____

_____

_____

In loving memory of Bubba and Luker.

*And, special thanks
to the Midtown Animal Clinic, Davis, California,
for allowing us to photograph their fine clinic (page 17).*